The Criminal Use of
False Identification

Loompanics Unlimited
Port Townsend, Washington

Published by:
Loompanics Unlimited
PO Box 1197
Port Townsend, WA 98368

Printed in U.S.A.

ISBN: 0-915179-05-9

THE CRIMINAL USE OF FALSE IDENTIFICATION

A Summary Report on the Nature, Scope, and Impact of False ID Use in the United States with Recommendations to Combat the Problem

NOVEMBER 1976

The Report of the Federal Advisory Committee on False Identification

UNITED STATES DEPARTMENT OF JUSTICE

ACKNOWLEDGEMENTS

The Committee Chairman gratefully acknowledges all those who have contributed to this Report, particularly Deputy Attorney General Harold R. Tyler, Jr., Assistant Attorney General Richard L. Thornburgh, Deputy Assistant Attorney General John C. Keeney, General Crimes Section Chief Alfred L. Hantman, Former Section Chief Carl W. Belcher; Douglas H. Westbrook of the Criminal Division, Emil Schroeder, FBI who originally presented the false identification problem to the Criminal Division; Deputy Director William F. Duggan of the Passport Office who spent hundreds of hours working on this project; Staff Director Dr. Thomas P. Kabaservice of the MITRE Corporation whose professionalism produced the final work product; Joseph Kochanski of the Law Enforcement Assistance Administration who coordinated LEAA's contribution to the Committee; and the Committee's 80 members and friends who contributed 18 months of their time and effort as volunteers.

ABSTRACT

The criminal use of false identification is a national problem with a multi-billion dollar impact on government, business, and the general public. In November 1974 the U.S. Attorney General established the Federal Advisory Committee on False Identification (FACFI) to assess the problem and recommend solutions. With MITRE support, the FACFI conducted surveys and examined the extent of false ID use in six major problem areas: drug smuggling, illegal immigration, fugitives from justice, fraud against business, fraud against government, and other criminal activity. The Committee ranked potential solutions in these areas by criteria that included not only an assessment of effectiveness but also an evaluation of possible impact on public convenience and privacy. This report contains the findings, background material, recommendations, and plans for implementation of the proposed solutions of the FACFI, and the appendices offer a comprehensive archive of current information available on the problem.

July 25, 1976

Mr. David Muchow, Chairman,
Federal Advisory Committee on False Identification,
Department of Justice,
Washington, D.C.

Dear Mr. Muchow:

I was very interested in your work on false identification. Here at the (deleted) Department of Motor Vehicles we issue drivers licenses and I.D. cards all day. You have no idea what goes on.

Birth certificates are accepted without anything to connect them with the bearer. If he says it is his, that is final. Uncertified photostats are accepted as conclusive, and you know what can be done with any document in a photostat machine. In the case of a female, only the first name need match, as she says she is married.

We see the same faces getting licenses and I.D. cards in different names all the time; for the purposes of welfare fraud, and illegal alien fraud.

Why do we do nothing? Because all employees are terrified of courtesy complaints. The attitude of supervision is, "Don't rock the boat; your job is to issue." Employees who expose fraud in identity face real, and I mean _real_ trouble. Avoiding courtesy complaints is the formost aim of the Department, and always was.

We are keeping our fingers crossed for you and your group. We have no interest but seeing this farce corrected.

If it were known who wrote this to you, the Department would try to bring dismissal charges against me, civil service notwithstanding; and therefore I cannot sign this letter. Please believe we are almost all fed up with what is happening.

Sincerely and best wishes,

(Signed with an X)

CONTENTS

Background and Membership of the FACFI ... 1

PART I: A Look at the Problem 5

PART II: Task Force Reports 49

    Government Payments 51

    Commercial Transactions 79

    Fugitives 109

    Federal Identification Documents 127

    State and Local Identification Documents .. 171

BACKGROUND AND MEMBERSHIP OF THE FACFI

The Federal Advisory Committee on False Identification (FACFI) was formed in 1974. Its creation was a product of several converging trends:

- Federal, state and local law enforcement agencies were being deluged with a host of new false identification techniques. Criminals and fugitives were using these techniques to perpetrate crimes and avoid arrest. Underground pamphlets such as the *Paper Trip* detailed steps for defrauding the public, while printing presses cranked out counterfeit "official" documents such as birth certificates and driver's licenses and advertised them for sale in interstate commerce.

- There was a growing concern on the part of citizens and public interest groups that false identification could be used for unauthorized access to confidential information, and that privacy was being invaded when criminals used innocent persons' names to commit crimes.

- The growing mobility of Americans required a more secure system of identifying strangers in commercial transactions such as cashing checks and using credit cards.

- The public was becoming more concerned over disclosures that millions of illegal aliens were entering the country, rampant fraud in government social welfare programs was coming to light, and innumerable other crimes involving false identification were increasing in number.

On September 15, 1973 and October 3, 1973, Miss Frances Knight, Director, and Mr. William Duggan, Deputy Director of the Passport Office, U.S. Department of State, testified on false identification before the Internal Security Subcommittee of the Senate Judiciary Committee.* Their testimony called attention to passport

---

*Hearing Before the Subcommittee to Investigate the Administration of the Internal Security Act of the Committee on the Judiciary, United States Senate, September 15, 1972, 92nd Congress 2d Session.

frauds and forgeries related to illegal narcotics trafficking and other crimes.

In the Fall of 1973, the Passport Office and the Federal Bureau of Investigation exchanged information concerning the increasing problem of false identification. These discussions led to an informal meeting among interested Federal agencies and others concerning the use of false identification. On May 10, 1974, a one-day conference of forty-four representatives from more than fifteen government agencies and other organizations was held at the FBI Academy, Quantico, Virginia. This meeting concluded with the unanimous recommendation that an interagency task force on false identification be formed to combat the problem.

In the Fall of 1974, the Criminal Division of the Department of Justice prepared the necessary charter documents to establish a Federal Advisory Committee on False Identification. On October 14, 1974, Attorney General William B. Saxbe officially announced its creation. In his address, the Attorney General made the following statement:

> False identification is a common denominator in a wide range of serious crimes. Let me cite a few examples.
>
> The Weatherman organization has taken credit for a number of terrorist bombings. False identification has been found on some of its members taken into custody. It appears that false identification may be a factor in the success of 23 others who have successfully eluded capture thus far.
>
> But false credentials can touch virtually every aspect of crime. They are frequently used by narcotics peddlers and by persons passing counterfeit checks and securities, by those who take part in bank swindles, and in Social Security and welfare frauds.
>
> Car thieves often use false identification, not only to thwart police, but to rent or lease cars which are then driven off and sold.
>
> The list of offenses could go on and on. They include widespread and costly frauds through the use of credit cards. And another growing problem is the use of false identification by

illegal aliens who insulate themselves from authorities as they settle into new jobs and new lives...*

The announcement of the formation of the Federal Advisory Committee on False Identification and its charter were published in the Federal Register of October 22, 1974.**The charter states the nature and purpose of this Committee are:

1. To identify, with the assistance of Federal, state, and local agencies, as well as representatives from the private sector and the public:
   (a) the various criminal techniques used to obtain false identification;
   (b) the types of persons committing such crimes; and
   (c) the nature and extent of such crimes including their impact upon the criminal justice system and commercial transactions such as check passing, credit card fraud, and the obtaining of fraudulent loans, securities, and other commercial paper.
2. To develop a coordinated Federal plan for meeting the threat which Executive Branch Agencies face from false identification. Such plan will include a discussion of closing any loopholes in existing Federal laws, regulations or procedures, and strengthening the enforcement of such laws, regulations and procedures.
3. To assist state and local law enforcement agencies and bureaus of vital statistics in developing effective measures to prevent the obtaining of false identification and its criminal use.
4. To provide Federal, state and local agencies a forum and mechanism for the exchange of information on false identification.

In its deliberations, the Committee sought not only to aid law enforcement agencies but also to protect personal privacy. As Deputy Attorney General Harold R. Tyler, Jr. stated to the Committee:

---

*Address by William B. Saxbe, Columbus, Ohio, October 14, 1974.

**The Committee was chartered pursuant to the Federal Advisory Committee Act of 1972 (P.L. 92-463, Oct. 6, 1972).

> ... this is the very purpose of your Committee: to recommend law enforcement methods which are compatible with every citizen's vital right to reasonable privacy and fair treatment.*

The first meeting of the FACFI was held on November 14, 1974 in the Department of Justice, and monthly meetings were held thereafter. All of its meetings were open to the general public and all voting in the Committee was done by a consensus of those present, including members of the public.

Because of the extensive scope of the problem, the FACFI was divided into five Task Forces, each dealing with a different phase of the false identification problem:

Task Force I—Government Payments
Task Force II—Commercial Transactions
Task Force III—Fugitives
Task Force IV—Federal Identification Documents
Task Force V—State and Local Identification Documents.

FACFI membership consisted of representatives of government agencies at Federal, state and local levels, law enforcement officials, business groups such as the American Bankers Association, and members of the general public. All were volunteers and received no travel funds or remuneration for their assistance. Many independent business firms provided voluntary support to the Committee by sending observers to meetings and by contributing valuable technical background information.

In October 1975, The MITRE Corporation was retained under contract with the Department of Justice to act as technical and editorial staff to the FACFI. MITRE support included: assisting us in gathering additional data covering gaps in the initial FACFI surveys to determine the nature and scope of the false identification problem; surveying the state of the art in technology areas that dealt with potential solutions to the false identification problem; compiling a set of potential solutions to be voted upon and revised by the FACFI; conducting other technical research; and drafting the FACFI final report.

---

*Address by Harold R. Tyler, Jr., to the Federal Advisory Committee on False Identification, May 8, 1975.

PART I:
A Look at the Problem

CONTENTS

SECTION I — INTRODUCTION 7

SECTION II — THE SCOPE OF THE PROBLEM 12
    Effect on Society 13
    Definitions 15

SECTION III — COMMON IDENTIFICATION
DOCUMENTS 17
    Birth Certificate 17
    Driver's License 20
    U.S. Passport 21
    U.S. Visa and Alien ID Card 22
    Social Security Card 23
    Selective Service Draft Card 24
    Voter Registration Card 24
    Credit Cards 25
    Non-Government ID 26

SECTION IV — FRAUDULENT ID USE 27
    Drug Smuggling 29
    Illegal Immigration 30
    Fugitives from Justice 32
    Fraud Against Business 33
        Check Forgery and Fraud 33
        Credit Card Fraud 36
        Securities Fraud 38
        Embezzlement 40
    Fraud Against Government 41
        Welfare Fraud 42
        Social Security Fraud 46
    Other Criminal Activity 47

SECTION 1

AN INTRODUCTION

Around 5,000 years ago, when primitive man began to domesticate animals, he introduced the concept of using possessions such as rings and axes for "exchange" goods. Previously, he bartered what goods he had for those he wanted. Four thousand years later, the Chinese issued the first paper money, and five hundred years ago banking and paper currency were developed further in Europe.

Today, the exchange of goods and money is a sophisticated process of symbol manipulation in computerized transactions on an international scale. American society -- 215 million strong in 1975 -- participates in this increasingly complex socio-economic system in ways that are markedly different than even twenty-five years ago.

In the past when a person gave "goods for goods" or accepted currency in exchange for his goods or services, he depended to a large extent on two safeguards against criminal incursion in these transactions:

- Personal knowledge of the person with whom he transacted, and

- Reliance on the legitimacy of the medium of exchange.

In today's society, both of these safeguards have been disrupted because of the:

- Transient nature of the population, and

- Necessity of relying on paper substitutes (e.g., checks, credit cards, signature on application) whose legitimacy is not guaranteed.

The modern businessman or government employee does not usually know with whom he deals. Unlike his counterpart in earlier days (who personally checked the teeth of his animal purchase, bit the gold coin, or carefully examined the legal tender) he accepts a substitute, the authenticity of which along with its bearer he has limited ability to verify.

Alvin Toffler in <u>Future Shock</u> states that "Between March 1967 and March 1968 -- in a single year -- 36,600,000 Americans (not counting children less than one year) changed their place of residence." Members of this mobile population do not know each other in the same way that was once common. When we move, we must carry our identity in the papers we have accumulated that "prove" who we are.

This significant shift in our manner of transacting has not eluded the notice of the criminal element, present in all societies, who find ways to use the prevailing system to their own ends. An "underground" press has published a do-it-yourself manual entitled <u>The Paper Trip</u> whose advice confirms how much the paper identities we carry from city to city have become the currency of fraud, proliferating at an alarming rate. If our dollar currency were being counterfeited at an equal rate, the impact would be obvious and startling, both to the economy and to the general public confidence. However, the increase in the use of false ID to "buy" goods, services, entry into the country, and shelter from prosecution is much harder to detect.

From <u>The Paper Trip</u>:

> Everywhere one goes, to prove he's 'somebody', he has to present the appropriate document or card which says he actually is that person. His 'identification', or ID makes him that person. Amazing, right? Well not really. ....American society is no longer a people society, but a PAPER society....

The paper says who you are, not you. Actually, of course, you do know who you are, but you don't want the paper telling you who you are. The solution? The Paper Trip!

Figure 1. Cover of Underground Publication The Paper Trip

The manual continues with such rhetoric and then outlines, step by step, how one may obtain many false identities and use them for fraudulent purposes. For example, the authors inform their readers that with a false ID:

> You can rent a car, never pay more than the initial fee, and drive it all the way across the country and back without paying for more than gas and oil. Use good ID and simply leave the car somewhere after the trip. You disappear. This is not car theft, either.

Such techniques were presented in another underground paper called "Gemini Gallery" in which an article proposed "How to Disappear Completely and Start a New Life with a Brand New Identity." Advertisements such as this also appear:

Figure 2. Advertisement on Securing a New Identity

Such disappearing acts are, indeed, not so fantastic. Journalist David Black tried out many of the methods proposed by The Paper Trip and documented the ease with which he established himself in a community under a false identity. Interviews on the CBS television show "60 Minutes," broadcast on February 1, 1976, provided further documentation of how false ID fraud is perpetrated. A CBS researcher posed on camera as an imposter who successfully obtained and used a complete set of false IDs.

The means do exist to create a false identity in order to commit a crime. Finding out just how big the problem of false identification has become nationwide has been the task of the FACFI. The FACFI has sampled the accumulated experience of officials in Federal and state government, law enforcement, and the business community in order to define the full scope of the problem.

We have found clear evidence of widespread abuses in identification documents commonly used in our society. These abuses not only subject the public to a grievous and illegal "tax" through the fraud committed, they also undermine the trust among individuals upon which our commercial and governmental institutions depend.

SECTION 2

THE SCOPE OF THE PROBLEM

The work of the FACFI represents the first serious study of the illegal use of both bona fide and counterfeit documents. We have, therefore, extended our investigation in as much breadth and depth as possible in order to reveal the full impact of the problem in the U.S. Questions of the economic, social and legal effects on the populace were addressed with a view to protecting society from criminal abuse and to making recommendations for safeguards against further abuse. The Committee in this undertaking was dealing with the delicate relationship of Federal and state jurisdictions as well as Privacy Acts and the underlying principle of maintaining the freedoms of an open society. We wished to find answers to such questions as:

- Who is affected by false ID use?

- How big is the problem?

- Where are financial losses incurred as a result of false identification?

- Which are the most significant problem areas?

- Are crimes of violence as well as those of an economic nature aided by false identification? To what extent?

- What state and Federal laws now exist regarding ID use?

- What state, Federal, or technical safeguards against false ID use already exist? How effective are they?

- What are possible solutions to the problem?

- Which solutions do we recommend?

In finding answers to these questions, the FACFI has begun to uncover a serious problem of considerable import.

EFFECT ON SOCIETY

The criminal use of false identification documents represents a multibillion dollar problem in the United States. False identification is costing American business well over $1 billion per year. Most of this loss is related to check fraud and counterfeiting, but significant additional losses occur in the areas of credit card fraud and theft of securities and other negotiable instruments. Our estimates of the extent of the effects on business are based on the best available data but should not be considered as complete. The individual citizen pays for the cost of false ID crime against business, primarily in increased cost of goods and services. When small businesses fail because of the particularly severe fraud losses they encounter the consumer also suffers in terms of loss of choice.

The use of a false ID to obtain welfare or other social benefits, to import illegal drugs, or to maintain one's status as an illegal alien or fugitive has a devastating dollar impact on government at all levels. The success of such activities not only results in direct and indirect costs to taxpayers but also undermines public confidence in government.

Our findings indicate that an individual in our society, in addition to his legal tax burden, pays an additional illegal tax in the form of fraudulent payments and services to users of false IDs committing fraud against government. In New York City, for example, the cost of providing welfare benefits and municipal services has exceeded the resources available from taxpayers. The Immigration and Naturalization Service has estimated that over 10% of New York's population -- about one million persons -- are illegal aliens. Through the use of false identification, it is probable that these aliens are enjoying either employment or welfare benefits to which they are not entitled. While we cannot yet make accurate estimates of the national impact of these crimes on the individual taxpayer, we would emphasize that the burden of this type of crime is felt by citizens nationwide.

Congress has already been apprised of the false identification problem. The <u>Congressional Record</u> of June 28, 1973, March 5, 1974, and most recently of December 5, 1975 carried warnings of false ID fraud, especially as it is perpetrated in the receipt of welfare benefits and illegal entry into the U.S. Frances Knight, Director of the Passport Office sees investigation of and action on the problem as long overdue. She states that "The Passport Office has been ringing the alarm on passport and identification fraud for 43 years."

Although false identification has been an area of concern for a long time, current incidents point to growing abuse. Not only have the statistics proven to be extensive in scope, but individual cases have demonstrated blatant and expensive abuse. For example, Miss Knight continues:

> Investigators probing Chicago welfare frauds uncovered one case which must be near the top in sheer gall and ingenuity: a thirty-one count fraud indictment charged a welfare recipient with the receipt of illegal welfare benefits, medical assistance, food stamps, in addition to Social Security and Veterans benefits from four non-existent spouses.... The recipient of all these benefits used 80 different names; 30 different addresses and 15 different telephone numbers. The total annual benefits received by this one person was estimated at a minimum of $150.000 annually in cash assistance alone.

Added to such losses are those connected with false ID use in other areas. False IDs can be used to:

- Illegally enter institutions of higher learning.
- Collect re-enlistment bonuses from the military services.
- Take entrance exams and tests for unqualified students.
- Escape prosecution or apprehension.
- Gain entry into homes for robbery or crimes of violence.
- Practice a profession under false credentials.

The public is the true victim of the growing menace of false ID use.

DEFINITIONS

Certain definitions were agreed upon for this report. We define false identification fraud as the intentional use by an individual of a document containing a name or personal attributes other than his own for the purpose of assisting in the commission of a crime or in avoiding the legal consequences of a previous crime. This definition is broad enough to encompass the use of a forged check to obtain cash or other benefits, even if no supporting documentation is demanded by the victim of this transaction. However, it does not include simple not-sufficient-funds (NSF) fraud in which an individual presents a check against an existing account in his true name with the knowledge that the check will not clear. Our definition also includes the use of false identification documents for non-criminal transactions by fugitives.

The Committee did consider the non-criminal use of false documents by citizens under certain circumstances, such as the necessity of an individual to establish a "cover" to avoid reprisals from organized crime or a hostile foreign power. Within its charter, however, this was not a primary area of the Committee's investigation.

There are adequate legal channels in such cases for obtaining identtification documents in a new name.

Included as an identification document (ID) were many types of documents whose intended or major purpose is not identification of the bearer. These include government checks and credit cards, as well as commonly used IDs such as birth certificates, driver's licenses, passports, employee identification badges, and military identification cards. Any of these documents can be used to support a fraudulent claim to an identity. For purposes of classification we have defined three fundamental methods of using an identification document for false purposes.

- Alteration refers to the abuse of a legitimate document by changing significant identification elements, such as the name, photograph, age, or physical description of the legitimate bearer.

- Counterfeiting refers to the unauthorized creation of a complete document by an unauthorized source to support a false identification. For our purposes, counterfeiting includes the unauthorized use of a genuine blank official form to create a false ID.

- Imposture refers to the use of another person's (living or deceased) legal documents as one's own, such as presenting a deceased person's birth certificate to apply for a driver's license.

SECTION 3

COMMON IDENTIFICATION DOCUMENTS

The United States does not have a unique document that can be used to verify the identity of the bearer. Because of the frequent need for such verification in employment and commercial transactions, several types of documents not designed for such use have become de facto identification documents. The birth certificate, which is legal proof of only age, place of birth, parentage and citizenship of the named individual, is extensively used in employment and in applications for benefits or for obtaining other documents. The state-issued driver's license has become indispensable as an identification document for many commercial transactions; for this reason, many states now issue special "licenses" to non-drivers and blind persons. Several other documents issued by government agencies and private sources also serve as de facto identification documents.

This section summarizes the various types of common identification documents that are used either as primary IDs to defraud or gain access or benefits, or as breeder documents for obtaining further identification to use or falsify.

BIRTH CERTIFICATE

Birth certificates in the United States are generally kept in local vital records offices, over 7,000 of which are authorized to issue certified copies of birth certificates. (Only in a few states are birth certificates issued exclusively at the state level.) Approximately 10 million certified copies of birth certificates are issued each year, and over 80 percent of those requested are received and processed by mail. The name and return address of the requestor are usually the only indications of the requestor's identity.

There are no uniform standards for either the form of the document or for processing requests for certified copies. A request may legally be made for a copy of another person's birth certificate if the requester is related to the individual or has legitimate need for the document. Some states and Washington, D.C. regard all vital records as public documents, a copy of which must be supplied to any interested person. We have found no state law that authorizes a registry official to refuse to honor an unsigned request for a birth certificate.

Under these conditions, an imposter can quite easily acquire a certified copy of the birth certificate of a person, and this certificate can then be used to obtain additional IDs in the name of the person whose identity the imposter assumes. Frequently an imposter will choose to assume the identity of a person born about the same time as himself but who died in early childhood. This way of obtaining false identification -- called the Infant Death Identity (IDI) method --is difficult to detect because state birth and death records are largely uncorrelated and an imposter's identity is unlikely to be challenged. To apply for a copy of a birth certificate an imposter needs only the date, place of birth and names of the parents of a deceased person. This information can be obtained either from a death certificate (found by browsing in a local vital records office) or from newspaper accounts of a person's death. The process of obtaining and using false identification by the IDI method is illustrated in Figure 3.

Immigration and Naturalization officials have documented many false claims to citizenship, many of which used the IDI method of obtaining false documents. They relate, for example, the case of an illegal alien wanted for homicide in the Phillipines who created several new identities for himself in California using the records of deceased U.S. citizens. He also used the IDI method to obtain fraudulent birth certificates and U.S. passports for at least 12 other illegal aliens, charging fees of up to $2000 for this service before being apprehended.

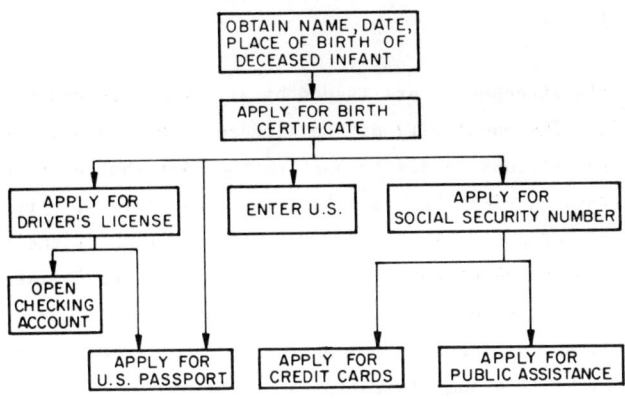

Figure 3. The IDI Method

Although application for certified copies by imposters appears to be the most significant abuse of the birth certificate, counterfeit and altered certificates have also been used in false identification frauds. Counterfeiting is aided by the fact that forms of birth certificates and authenticating seals vary widely in the U.S.; over 1,000 different forms may be found of presently issued certified copies. Counterfeit documents can be obtained from underground printers and are difficult to detect if the corresponding legitimate document is not secure against photocopying. Documents altered to change date of birth or to invent an additional "dependent" for tax or welfare purposes are less common. Erasure and inexpensive photocopying are the methods usually attempted. Genuine blank forms and even official seals are sometimes used to create counterfeit certificates. Theft of blank forms or misuse by dishonest employees is made easy in some states by the lack of strict security and accounting procedures for blank forms.

DRIVER'S LICENSE

Driver's licenses are issued by all 50 states and the District of Columbia. The popularity of the license as a credential for business transactions is due in part to the fact that a driver's license always carries the bearer's signature, address, birth date, and some type of physical description. A photograph of the legal bearer is used on 36 of the 51 types of U.S. license; 46 carry the bearer's height, 40 weight, 36 color of eyes, and 18 color of hair. The bearer's Social Security number (SSN) is collected and maintained in the Motor Vehicle Administration's record system in 31 states. In eleven jurisdictions the SSN serves as the license number; however, under the provisions of the Privacy Act this use of the Social Security number cannot be extended to record systems not using the SSN prior to January 1, 1975.

Forty-four jurisdictions claim to seek positive proof of full name, date, and birthplace of an applicant prior to issuance of an initial driver's license; however, such proof may be waived if the applicant presents a valid license from another state. A birth certificate is always accepted as proof; some states, however, accept school records, military ID, or a baptismal certificate as well. Thirty-three states presently issue an identification card (usually in the same form as a driver's license) to non-drivers; in four of these states, a birth certificate or similar proof of age and birthplace is not required to obtain such a card.

Since the birth certificate is accepted as "proof" of identity in applying for a driver's license, a false birth certificate can be used to obtain a license in the same false name. Counterfeit documents that are often good enough to pass close visual inspection are also legally available from "underground" sources. Because the form and content of a driver's license varies, detection of a counterfeit out-of-state license by merchants or local police is extremely difficult. False application and counterfeiting

20

appear to be the most common forms of abuse of driver's licenses.
Twenty-nine types of driver's licenses incorporate measures that
resist attempts at alteration; however, none are foolproof and some
are still too easily altered.

U.S. PASSPORT

Passports , which are essential for international travel, can
be used for either legitimate purposes or such illegal purposes
as drug smuggling. By definition, a passport attests to the identity
and citizenship of its bearer; therefore, specific evidence of
identity and citizenship is required from a passport applicant. A
birth certificate is usually the accepted proof of citizenship;
identity can be established either by a government-issued photo ID
(such as a driver's license) or by affidavit of a witness who knows
the applicant personally. Applications must be submitted in person
before a passport agent or other authorized official. After a
waiting period of several days, the completed passport is delivered
by mail or may be picked up in person by the applicant.

Because in almost all cases of passport fraud there is
false ID use, the Passport Office has been concentrating on
alleviating this problem. When in 1972 the number of passport
frauds detected in the United States rose sharply, from 174 in 1971
to 288 in 1972, the Passport Office initiated a fraud detection program. As a result of this program, the Passport Office increased
its ability to detect fraud in the application stage (as opposed
to detection upon arrest) from 28% of reported cases in 1973 to 53%
in 1975. The number of domestic passport frauds detected by all
methods for fiscal year 1971 through 1975 increased: from 174 in 1971;
288 in 1972; 449 in 1973; 553 in 1974; to 617 in 1975. Detecting
these frauds upon application has helped keep down those criminal
activities, especially drug trafficking and illegal alien entry, that
are perpetrated through passport fraud.

U.S. VISA AND ALIEN ID CARD

A visa is a document issued by a host nation granting permission to an alien to enter the host nation. A U.S. immigrant visa permits the bearer to settle and work in the U.S. and eventually to apply for citizenship. An immigrant visa is generally issued to an alien who has either a close family relationship with a U.S. citizen or resident alien, or a profession or job skill that is in short supply in the U.S. The number of these visas granted each year is limited by law. Aliens who have neither family ties nor job skills sometimes participate in sham marriages or obtain fraudulent documents to get immigrant visas.

A U.S. nonimmigrant visa permits a temporary or limited stay (1) by a visitor on business or pleasure; (2) by a student; or (3) by any alien who has a residence abroad (that he does not intend to abandon) and who has sufficient funds to pay for the trip. Some nonimmigrant visa categories permit specific employment to aliens who are, for example, journalists, foreign government officials, trainees or artists; however, the validity of this type of visa depends on the alien's continuing the same work. An alien who is unable to obtain an immigrant visa often attempts to get a nonimmigrant visa by using fraudulent documents to misrepresent his reasons for visiting the U.S., his financial status or his employment. He also can buy a counterfeit visa or an altered passport that already contains a valid visa. Once in the U.S. he overstays his visa and becomes an illegal alien.

Both immigrant and nonimmigrant visas are issued by consular officers abroad; an immigration officer examines each entering alien's visa at the port of entry. Each immigrant is then given a Form I-151 a photo ID card which serves to identify him as a legal resident alien. When traveling outside the U.S. he uses this as evidence of his right to re-enter the U.S. An alien set on illegally entering the U.S. might use a stolen or counterfeited I-151, while an illegal alien already in the U.S. might use an I-151 to establish his identity as a legal resident alien.

Immigration officers also issue border crossing cards to permit Mexicans to visit the U.S. border area without a visa. Like the I-151, these photo ID cards are subject to counterfeiting and alteration to gain illegal entry into the U.S.

SOCIAL SECURITY CARD

Although never intended by the Social Security Administration to be used for personal identification, the Social Security card has become an important document in maintaining employment records and in obtaining other identification documents. Although the Social Security number is widely used for tax racords and as a driver's license number, it is neither unique nor protected against imposter use. The Social Security Administration estimates that over 4.2 million people have more than one SSN.

Prior to 1974, SSNs were issued in the name of any individual upon submission of an application form, in person or by mail, without any other evidence of identity. Evidence of identity, age, and citizenship of the applicant is now required. In recent testimony before Congress, an official of the Social Security Administration listed the kinds of documents that are acceptable in applying for an SSN. The list included several documents that are easily forged or obtained under false pretenses, i.e., baptismal certificate, library card, and voter registration card.

The Social Security card in its present form has no safeguards against counterfeiting. Unofficial "cards" are also available by mail from commercial suppliers. Ostensibly the reproductions are intended only to remind the cardholder of his SSN; however, the suppliers do not check the authenticity of SSNs provided by their customers, so the unofficial cards can be used to support a false identity.

SELECTIVE SERVICE DRAFT CARD

It is estimated that as many as thirty million draft cards were issued before the last one was sent out in 1975. Although they were issued only as a means of informing the individual of his classification or Selective Service number, they have been used as identification cards to prove age as well as for other uses for which they were not designed. The draft card is notoriously unsecure: it is merely a typed postcard; is unserialized; the background information at the application stage is largely unverified; it is easily forged; it contains no photograph; and its uses rarely, if ever, cause it to be scrutinized by the issuer.

VOTER REGISTRATION CARD

Voter registration cards are issued by local Boards of Election and are used by their holders as evidence of age and citizenship for limited purposes. For example, these cards are frequently presented by persons to support their claim of U.S. residence for re-entry from Canada and Mexico. However, they are not accepted as evidence of age and citizenship when applying for a U.S. passport, and are not usually accepted as part of a driver's license application. Limited investigation into voter registration procedures by FACFI staff suggests that these cards are very easy to obtain under false pretenses. Registration by mail is permitted in many jurisdictions, and even where a personal appearance is required, the only evidence of age, citizenship, residence, and identity of the registrant that can be demanded by local officials is a verbal declaration given under penalty of perjury. The ability of the local Board of Election to check any of the entitling data is typically very limited.

Since the voter registration card contains no physical description of the legitimate bearer, it can be used with relative ease by imposters. Voter registration cards are commonly used by aliens attempting illegal entry into the U.S. and have been sold to illegal aliens for this purpose at prices ranging up to $350.

CREDIT CARDS

Although a credit card contains certain printed and embossed information which, when checked by a merchant, may confirm the validity of the card, the primary means of cardholder authentication is the signature on the card. Normally no other ID is required to charge goods or services at a wide variety of retail outlets unless a question arises as to the validity of the card or the authenticity of the cardholder. Bank cards such as Master Charge and Bank Americard can even be used to obtain cash.

Credit cards are obtained by mailing an application form that requests credit information, but not information about identity; a credit and reference check is then made before issuing the card. Cards in a false name can be obtained by false application or by theft of legitimate cards from the mail or from cardholders. One article reported:

> Credit card thieves sometimes use the cards they steal but more often they peddle them in underworld circles. When the black market was at its height in New York, a thief would sell a card to a dealer for $25; the dealer in turn would dispose of it for as much as $150 if the card were 'clean' -- i.e., without a signature.

Although use by an imposter of a stolen credit card appears to be the most common form of abuse, obtaining credit cards in many identities is an equally serious abuse. One recent newspaper account told of a credit card fraud committed by <u>one person who had obtained 1,000 credit cards using 300 different false identities.</u>

NON-GOVERNMENT IDs

When a person applies for benefits or is establishing identity for other purposes, he sometimes uses privately-issued identification to reinforce other documentation. Privately-issued documents include baptismal certificates, student ID cards, employee badges, business cards and membership cards of all types. Baptismal certificates are sometimes accepted in lieu of birth certificates to establish age, e.g., of a dependent child. Such documents, however, are easily obtained or constructed fraudulently. Blank baptismal certificates are sometimes available at religious-goods or stationery stores, or can be obtained by mail. Commercial photo IDs can be made to order by photographic studios in every large city.

This non-government, unofficial ID was found to be the type most frequently used in the cashing of checks stolen from the mails. Business and membership cards can usually be obtained from job printers, and many employee badges, courtesy cards, and other types of unofficial ID can be easily counterfeited.

SECTION 4

FRAUDULENT ID USE

Crimes assisted by the use of one or several false IDs represent a significant national problem. Directly or indirectly, this problem affects every American household in terms of the cost of government benefits paid to imposters, the cost of fraud against business that is passed on to consumers, and the threat to public health and safety from drug smugglers and fugitives.

Possession of false identification documents gives a criminal, or someone intent on committing a crime, the means to appear and disappear almost at will and without a trace. Attempts in FACFI surveys to profile the typical user of false IDs were largely unsuccessful. As in the case of many types of fraud, successful perpetrators of false identification fraud are quite indistinguishable from the groups they pretend to represent. Thus, a request for a profile of the typical suspect of welfare fraud using false identification yielded the description of a young, unmarried, unemployed woman resident of a metropolitan area, which is in fact a description of a typical legitimate welfare mother as well. Similarly, the typical check forger can be described as a middle-aged male, which also describes a large percentage of legitimate check users.

The only exception we have found to the "invisibility" of false identification suspects occurs in passport fraud. Here the typical offender is usually an international traveler, 18 to 40 years of age, who does not travel with a family group or on government-related business. Since this description fits only 40% of the passport holders, the possibility exists of decreasing passport fraud to some degree by screening for user type in review of passport applications.

One further distinguishing characteristic has emerged of those involved in false identification fraud; suspects are more likely to be repeat offenders than is the average for criminals apprehended. For example, 76% of those arrested for forgery and counterfeiting in 1971 had previously been arrested for the same crime at least once; this compares with a recidivism rate of only 68% for overall crime.

The universality of the use of false IDs by criminals is unquestionable. A random sampling of 500 cases in which a fugitive was being sought by the FBI showed that in every case the fugitive was known to have used at least one alias. In 75 of these cases, the fugitives had previously been identified under five or more aliases, and in one case the subject is known to have used more than 30 different false identities.

Besides aiding drug smuggling, illegal immigration and fugitives from justice, the use of false IDs materially assists fraud involving stolen checks, credit cards, securities, and welfare and Social Security benefit checks. Although we cannot provide firm figures on the scope of government benefit checks stolen from the mails and subsequently cashed by forgery, the experience of state and local welfare departments suggests that such losses are in the order of hundreds of millions of dollars annually.

The U.S. Postal Inspection Service during FY 1974 received reports of 140,864 checks with a total face value of over $22 million stolen from the mails and subsequently cashed. A sampling of almost 6,000 of these checks was undertaken by postal inspectors to determine the type of false ID used to cash the checks. About 25% of the sampled cases were definitely determined to involve the use of a false ID other than the forged check itself (which becomes a false ID upon forgery). When cashing of a stolen check was supported by another ID, the one most commonly used was the commercial photo ID, followed in frequency by a stolen welfare ID and state driver's license.

This section presents data on the significant fraudulent uses nationally of false IDs. These findings are probably conservative because our studies are based only on those cases of false identification that have been detected. The crimes we illustrate would be much more difficult to commit if criminals did not have such easy access to false identification documents. Table 2 summarizes the extent of the problem in the six problem areas, discussed in more detail below, and lists the sources of information for this estimate.

Table 2

Summary of Scope and Impact of
National False Identification Problem

Problem Area	Scope of Problem	Extent of False ID Use	Sources of Data
Drug Smuggling	> $1 billion/yr.	80% of hard drugs smuggled	Customs Service, Drug Enforcement Administration, Passport Office
Illegal Immigration	> $12 billion/yr.*	Unknown; used in entry, employment, welfare application	Immigration & Naturalization Service, independent studies
Fugitives From Justice	> 300,000 fugitives/yr.	~ 100% of Federal cases	FBI, sheriffs and police survey
Fraud Against Business	> $3 billion/yr.†	> $1 billion/yr.	American Bankers Assoc., independent studies
Fraud Against Government	Unknown	Unknown	Surveys of Welfare officials, published studies
Other Criminal Activity	Unknown	Very common	FBI, sheriffs and police survey

> More than
* Estimated U.S. tax burden
† Includes out-of-pocket losses and cost of collection attempts

DRUG SMUGGLING

False identification is indispensable to the well-organized smuggling rings that carry in the bulk of the hard drugs supplied to U.S. addicts. Statistics compiled by the U.S. Customs Service and the Drug Enforcement Administration show that 80% of all hard drugs are imported by rings making extensive use of false IDs. One such group whose smuggling activities have been carefully studied is the Brotherhood of Eternal love. Between 1968 and 1973, this group alone is estimated to have smuggled 24 tons of hashish into the U.S. The principal means by which this group avoided

detection was by securing documents, such as U.S. passports, under
false names.

The activities of the Brotherhood of Eternal Love indicate the
extensiveness of false ID use for a solitary smuggling group. As
of October 1973, 130 separate passport frauds had been attributed
to members of this group; fifty-one of these frauds were accomplished
with counterfeit birth certificates. Indictments were obtained
against 25 individuals. The individual who was considered to be
the leader of the LSD operation was arrested on four separate
occasions under four different false identities; on each occasion
he escaped by posting and forfeiting relatively small bonds before his
true identity was discovered.

Accurate records of seizures of dangerous drugs by the U.S.
Customs Service were obtained for fiscal years 1967 through 1973.
In FY 1973, seizures involving well-organized rings using false IDs
totalled $100 million ("street value" at time of seizure). From
statements obtained by captured members of these rings, the value of
drugs successfully smuggled by these groups was estimated as $1 billion
in FY 1973, which does not include estimates of drugs smuggled by
unknown individuals or by individuals not using false IDs. Assuming
the level of smuggling as constant (though, in fact, its increase
is more likely), we conclude that a minimum of $1 billion each year
is being lost in illegal purchases of narcotics made available through
false identification. Such an estimate does not include the indirect
costs to society, such as the value of goods stolen by addicts to
purchase the drugs, the cost of programs to treat the addicts, or
their movement through the criminal justice system.

ILLEGAL IMMIGRATION

The most recent estimate of the number of illegal aliens
presently living in the U.S. is about 8 million, 6 million of whom
are adults. The U.S. Immigration and Naturalization Service believes

that the number of such illegal aliens is increasing at the rate of more than 250,000 per year. The net tax burden on the U.S. for each adult illegal alien is estimated in a recent study to be $2,000 per year. This estimate considers direct costs such as public services and welfare benefits to the extent they are not supported by taxes paid by the aliens and indirect costs related to the job displacement of U.S. citizens by illegal aliens. The tax burden does not include losses from tax evasion by aliens or balance of payments losses from funds sent out of the U.S. by illegal aliens. The total estimated tax burden from the presence of illegal aliens is thus estimated at over $12 billion for 1976.

The extent to which this staggering burden can be attributed to the use of false documents by illegal aliens is unknown but believed to be substantial and increasing. Over 15,000 illicit INS documents (border-crossing and alien registration cards) were encountered by INS personnel during fiscal 1975; these documents had been purchased in Mexico from document vendors and smuggling rings at a total cost of $1.7 million. The number of illicit documents seized is believed to be only a small fraction of those in use by illegal aliens. This belief has been supported by occasional large seizures of counterfeit forms and the fact that the black market price of such documents is declining steadily.

A study on the subject, the Fraudulent Entrants Study, which is part of the Major Illegal Alien Study being undertaken by INS during 1976, was recently completed by INS. This study indicated that in FY 1975 at least 14 times the routinely detected number of aliens with fraudulent alien documents successfully entered through Southwest border ports. Additionally, at least 10 times the routinely detected number of aliens falsely claiming U.S. citizenship along the Southwest border were successful in gaining admission. Together, these groups account for at least a quarter of a million illegal entries by the use of fraudulent documents or false verbal claims to U.S. citizenship

It is reasonable to assume that false claims to legal status or citizenship are used by illegal aliens in obtaining employment and welfare benefits to which they are not entitled, which contributes heavily to the estimated tax burden previously cited. The use of false documentation by illegal aliens is probably increasing because of the recent requirements for evidence of age, identity, and citizenship in applying for a Social Security number, and new state legislation restricting payment of welfare benefits to illegal aliens.

FUGITIVES FROM JUSTICE

Escaped prisoners and other dangerous fugitives almost always obtain false identification documents to avoid detection and capture. Members of militant groups such as the Black Liberation Army, Weather Underground, and Symbionese Liberation Army, who have gone underground to carry on their activities, make extensive use of false IDs. They have been able to escape arrest for violent crimes for considerable periods of time because of effective false identification. Figure 4 shows that false ID use, including the specific use of the IDI method previously mentioned, is common enough knowledge to be included in the public's comic strip lexicon.

STEVE ROPER by Allen Saunders and William Overgard, Courtesy of Field Newspaper Syndicate.

Figure 4. Dangerous Fugitives: Customers for False IDs

The number of fugitives from justice is considerable. Between 1973 and 1975 an average of approximately 160,000 "criminal wanted" records each year were entered into the National Crime Information Center (NCIC), but not all persons sought under fugitive warrants are entered into the NCIC. The Federal Bureau of Investigation in fiscal 1974 located 37,891 fugitives indicted on Federal offenses or for crimes involving interstate travel.

The major impact of the use of false identification by criminal fugitives cannot, however, be measured in the number of offenders or dollar losses. Its impact is felt more in the loss of public confidence in law enforcement caused by the success of notorious fugitives in maintaining their covert status and in the danger such fugitives pose to society. We have found that their success is critically dependent on the availability of false IDs. While we cannot estimate the cost of the use of false IDs by fugitives, we emphasize that the ability of dangerous criminals to move freely and undetected in society is a serious threat to public safety and police morale.

FRAUD AGAINST BUSINESS

Check Forgery and Fraud

In a nationwide survey of police and sheriff's departments fraudulent cashing of checks, either stolen from the mails or drawn on accounts bearing false names, was cited as the most common criminal use of false IDs. Bad checks have become a major cause of financial loss to banks, far exceeding the loss from robbery and burglary combined. This loss is due in great measure to the successful use of one or more complete sets of false IDs that are part of the usual working equipment of the experienced forger or check fraud artist. See Figure 5. A recently arrested check forger had in his possession 30 different birth certificates with which he had already obtained 15 driver's licenses, 17 Social Security cards, 11 checking accounts, 4 credit cards, and 10 miscellaneous IDs.

Figure 5. A Common Check Cashing Scene Could Really Be a "Bank Robbery" Aided By A False ID "Disguise"

In 1973, about 25 billion checks were written in the United States; of these, approximately 0.65% (one out of 150) failed to clear and were returned to the depositor. These "return items" amounted to 169 million checks returned in 1973, 25 million of which proved to be counterfeit or forged, representing false identification fraud. Since the average dollar amount of all bad checks is estimated to be around $30, total out-of-pocket losses from counterfeit or forged checks amounts to over $750 million. The cost of attempting to collect on these checks, which averages about $10 per check, must be added to this total. Thus, we estimate that the losses due to counterfeit and forged checks totalled approximately $1 billion in 1973. Since the number of checks written is increasing rapidly from year to year, these losses may be expected to increase, even if the rate of forgery and counterfeiting does not.

Check fraud hits particularly hard at retail food stores and small businesses. The U.S. Department of Commerce estimates that bad check losses for food transactions exceeded $450 million in 1974. The typical food store receives checks for 85% to 90% of its total sales and in addition often acts as a "bank" to cash payroll and government checks for customers. Bad check losses have been reported by members of the National Association of Food Chains and the Super Market Institute at about 0.04% of total sales; therefore, **a single** average food store, with an estimated sales volume of $60,000 per week, puts $240 per week or $12,500 per year in the hands of check thieves. About 60% of these losses appear to involve false identification fraud (forgery and counterfeiting), while 40% are uncollectible "not-sufficient-funds" cases. We do not count as losses the much larger number of returned checks on which collection is ultimately made.

According to a study conducted by the Small Business Administration, bad checks accounted for about 13% of all crime-related losses to business in 1967-1968. The small business suffers a loss rate (in percentage of profits) over 3 times the average of business in general and 35 times that reported for large businesses.

Banks take the loss on only about 5% to 7% of all bad checks; however, the dollar losses tend to average considerably higher than in other businesses. The principal form of fraud affecting banks is forgery of stolen checks, with counterfeit checks contributing significantly also. The American Bankers Association estimates bank losses due to forgeries in 1974 at $50 million. Even though the direct loss is suffered by the first acceptor of the check rather than the bank, banks and their depositors suffer indirect losses as the result of bad checks, such as the cost of investigating incidents.

A survey conducted of 1974 losses to banks resulting from individuals presenting false identification for various bank activities revealed significant losses per crime. The average loss to the banks from checks cashed through the use of false IDs was $216, while the average for cashing savings bonds was $643. However, banks were much harder hit by the use of false IDs in opening new checking and/or savings accounts; total funds lost in this activity were $3,734,521 with an average per crime of $6,586. Most of these crimes were committed with falsified driver's licenses, the form of identification most often used in bank transactions. The Insurance and Protection Division of the American Bankers Association believes this survey "has verified the long-held belief of bankers and law enforcement officials that phony driver's licenses are the most prevalent means of false identification used to defraud banks."

Credit Card Fraud

Credit card transactions have continued to grow in volume; the gross billings of the two largest bank credit card associations (Bank Americard and Master Charge) reached $17.6 billion in 1974. Losses to business can occur as a result of three types of false identification fraud using such cards: misuse of a lost or stolen card by an imposter, use of a counterfeit card, or application for a card by a person with criminal intent. These losses may affect either the issuer of the card or the merchant accepting it, depending on circumstances.

A 1974 U.S. Department of Commerce publication placed losses on bank credit cards from all sources at approximately $500 million per year. Sources of specific estimates on credit card fraud losses have been limited, but the Committee has receive helpful information in the application area from the Fraud Application Section of the Western States Bankcard Association.

Formed in January 1975, the Association's unit may be the only investigative one of its kind devoted exclusively to identifying and combatting fraudulent applications in the credit card industry.

G. Pat Bland, Agent in Charge of the Section, describes the numerous well-organized groups they found operating in California with ties to other states

> These organizations are involved in the establishment of phoney credit files, loan fraud of all types and phoney businesses, some of which go so far as to file articles of incorporation to further their devious ends. Most of the better organized groups utilize fraudulent identification to insure success in their ventures. One such business averaged in excess of $5,000 per month in deposits on Master Charge Cards that were all obtained in fraud applications.

Individual cases investigated by the Fraud Application Section included one suspect, wanted for murder, who had used 37 identities, and another who victimized a California bank for $26,000 in four months with only _two_ cards. The examples uncovered by the Association seem to be only a part of a much larger incidence level. Bland continues:

> Our statistics show an increase in caseload during this first year of 673% over 1974. Initially, our average loss per case was approximately $2,800. After our first year of operation, we had reduced this average loss to $405 per identified fraud application.

He notes that the most measureable results are obtained when they have total participation by the credit industry.

The experience and information being accumulated by this group verifies the FACFI's estimation of the vast amounts of fraud that have yet to be uncovered, especially in areas such as credit card fraud, where virtually no reliable data has been forthcoming until now. The Association feels that "there are literally thousands of fraud applicants in California alone, and in their opinion, the same situation exists in every major metropolitan area in the nation."

Securities Fraud

False identification fraud makes up only a portion of the actual or potential fraud losses in the securities industry; many reports on securities fraud do not distinguish between potential and actual losses, much less between false identification fraud and other types of crime. It is therefore necessary to define carefully terms used to describe securities losses in order to eliminate confusion introduced by widely differing loss estimates contained in various reports.

The FACFI is specifically concerned with the value of lost, stolen or counterfeited securities that are negotiated through the use of false IDs. Because they represent ownership of value, securities certificates are of interest to criminal elements as much as cash or checks. If the securities are "bearer documents," that is certificates which are not registered and imprinted with the name of a specific owner, they are negotiable by anyone and the bearer is assumed to be the legal owner. Bearer certificates do not require the use of an ID for negotiation; therefore, false identification would not be necessary for their negotiation by a criminal. Registered certificates bear upon their face the name of the owner of record, are legally negotiable only by the owner of record, and are therefore similar to checks, in that some measure of fraud is necessary to transfer ownership without consent of the rightful owner. This fraud may take the form of alteration of the certificate or use of false ID in an attempt to impersonate the owner of record.

A "risk of loss" to the financial industry arises when securities are lost or stolen; the risk equals the value of those securities. An "actual loss" occurs only when lost or stolen securities are converted to cash. Although an owner of securities incurs a loss when bearer certificates are lost or stolen, he can replace registered certificates. Loss may still be suffered by the financial industry if registered certificates are fraudulently negotiated. Negotiation may be accomplished by direct conversion to cash through sale or use of the certificates as collateral to secure a loan. We are concerned only with the cases of actual loss resulting from securities which are lost, stolen, or counterfeited and subsequently negotiated through the use of fales ID; data collected from the sources mentioned below were evaluated in the light of this concern.

In 1973, testimony before the Permanent Subcommittee on Investigations, the Committee on Government Operations, of the U.S. Senate included the statement by Mr. W. Henry duPont that "...it is our considered judgment that the dollar value of lost, missing and stolen Government, state, municipal and corporate securities could be as high as $50 billion". This figure was based on information from an estimated 1% of the total number of handlers of securities. No basis was established to validate the extrapolation, to define the risk of loss, actual loss, or applicability of false ID to this figure.

The U.S. Marshals' Service, on the basis of a 1974-1975 survey of 287 banking institutions, stated that during the three-year period 1971-1973, 11 incidents of stolen or fraudulent securities representing a dollar loss of $5,136,554 were reported. Loss in that report was equated only to risk of loss as defined above.

Neither actual loss nor false ID involvement were addressed specifically.

In a report of a survey conducted by The New York Stock Exchange entitled the "Magnitude of Lost and Stolen Securities in N.Y.S.E. Member Firms 1969-1972," the market value of lost or stolen securities reported to the N.Y.S.E. Stock Clearing Corporation ranged from a low of $4.6 million in 1973 to a high of $14.7 million in 1970. Data from all reporting organizations to the N.Y.S.E. Stock Clearing Corporation ranged from a low of $24.1 million in 1972 to $104 million in 1973. Since these figures do not specifically address actual loss or the extent to which false identification may have been involved, they are of little direct value to FACFI.

The National Association of Securities Dealers (NASD), Inc., conducted a survey of its membership convering the period 1972-1974 that attempted to cover the specific area of false identification. Replies from 2,734 respondents, representing an almost 90% response, reported 44 distinct cases of loss "...incurred vis-a-vis counterfeit securities and/or a return to the marketplace of securities previously obtained through some forms of misappropriation". The value of this loss was reported as $563,412.

Since the NASD survey specifically addressed the area of concern to the FACFI, the information reported therein appears to be the best indication of the scope of the false ID problem in securities fraud.

Embezzlement

Embezzlement is another area in which fraud against business may be perpetrated. While the majority of embezzlers operate under their true name, the potential of infiltration of business firms by employees hired under false identities should not be overlooked. In 1974, the Washington, D.C. Metropolitan Police Department investigated twenty-two cases of embezzlement in which the suspect was found to be using a false ID. These cases represented 15% of all complaints for embezzlement handled by the Department in 1974. The average loss to business from each reported incident was about $3,000.

Banks and other credit grantors are also subjected to large losses through embezzlement by persons making loans with false identification. Typically, this type of fraud involves a dishonest bank officer who processes loans for a confederate posing as a legitimate borrower. However, the "borrower" cannot be located when the loan falls due.

Another type of loan fraud is accomplished by a criminal's creating excellent credit ratings in the names of fictitious persons through the internal manipulation of the data banks of credit-reporting services. Participants in these loan fraud schemes acquire complete sets of false IDs to match their bogus credit ratings. A single bank victimized by one such scheme lost $200,000 in loans on nonexistent cars made to borrowers with false identification.

These "nonexistent borrower" schemes have been blamed for a major part of the $188 million fraud and embezzlement losses reported by financial institutions in fiscal year 1975. Total losses to all credit grantors from false ID credit swindles may never be known because such losses can be unwittingly written off as simple bad debts. The effectiveness of false identification in removing all traces of the perpetrator often makes it difficult for victimized businesses or prosecutors to sustain a fraud complaint.

FRAUD AGAINST GOVERNMENT

We have found that most state and national social welfare programs are very vulnerable to false identification fraud. Such fraud may take various forms -- applying for benefits under several identities, claiming nonexistent dependents, or in the case of Social

Security programs, claiming to be a dependent of a covered wage earner. No uniform standards exist for verifying the identity of claimants for benefits; in fact, some states do not require any identification.

In a recent case of welfare fraud in Denver, a woman was accused of using four different names to collect almost $50,000 in welfare money and food stamps over a four-year period. According to Orlando Romero, Director of the Denver Department of Social Services, it is difficult to know if fraud on this large a scale is happening more often than the Department is able to detect with present procedures and limited personnel. Romero admits, "I'm scared to death this is happening in other cases."

Misappropriation of benefits by imposters, usually with stolen welfare or Social Security checks or stolen food stamps, is another way in which fraud is committed with the aid of a false ID. The studies in New York City and Philadelphia, mentioned previously, revealed that 30% to 40% of all welfare checks reported "lost or stolen" were subsequently cashed by forgers. The annual loss in both cities from this kind of fraud reaches multimillion dollar proportions.

Welfare Fraud

Our surveys have shown that, due to the lack of identification standards for welfare recipients, neither Federal nor state agencies have a very good idea who is receiving almost $37 billion per year in public assistance and Social Security payments.
We have, therefore, no way to accurately estimate the scope of multiple collection of benefits by individuals using several identities. In fact, several welfare officials have admitted that there is no organized procedure for detecting such fraud; however, we have noted that institution of a photo ID program for welfare recipients in New York City in 1973 resulted in the closing of about 3,000 cases of in-

eligibility. These closings produced a saving of $7.2 million per year, which represented about 0.6% of all New York City assistance payments for FY 1974. It seems likely that a large portion of these cases represented multiple payments, since the only major change in procedure was the issuance of a photo ID to recipients.

Although many attempts at false identification fraud may have been discouraged by the photo ID program, the problem has not been eliminated. For example, after the Queens County (New York City) District Attorney found several cases of multiple applications for benefits under false names in a single welfare center, he declared in early 1975 that this type of fraud is "...the most serious problem faced in the administration of Public Assistance and one for which there are no present adequate safeguards...".

Cashing stolen or forged welfare checks is a major problem for which the FACFI has also received data from the Philadelphia and New York City studies. Before a determined effort was made in 1974 to reduce mailing of welfare checks, an average of 10,000 replacements for checks reported lost or stolen were issued each month in Philadelphia alone. About 41% of the checks reported lost or stolen were subsequently forged, resulting in an annual loss of approximately $4.8 million. This figure represents about 16% of the total public welfare budget in Philadelphia for the year 1972.

In New York City, over 30% of checks for which replacements were issued were subsequently cashed fraudulently. The total value of checks replaced in the year ending October 1973 was $28 million; therefore, losses through fraud amounted to at least $8.4 million for the year, which represents approximately 0.7% of total welfare payments in New York City for FY 1974. The acceptor of a forged check, rather than the issuer, is legally responsible for the loss; in practice, however, the process of recovery for welfare check losses is so slow and uncertain that the taxpayers, in fact, absorb most of the losses.

43

The food stamp program has expanded from modest beginnings to the point now where it encompasses 19.1 million recipients and a payment level of $5.2 billion per year. This program as presently structured provides a <u>disincentive</u> to investigation and prosecution of fraud in that such costs must be covered by the participating state, while all funds recovered must be returned to the Federal government. Not surprisingly, then, our data on false identification fraud in the food stamp program has been sparse. However, where local investigations have been pursued, significant evidence of false identification fraud has been uncovered. In North Pulaski County, Arkansas, which includes only 2.5% of all Arkansas food stamp cases, 57 cases of false identification fraud were recorded in one year. These cases carried a loss of nearly $19,000 in Federal funds, or about 2% of all food stamp funds expended in the county.

The sparseness of the data that has been received on false identification fraud in the area of welfare does not permit an accurate assessment of the national impact of this crime; however, the paucity of data does not mean that the problem is insignificant. False identification fraud has been discovered in significant proportions (1% to 2% of the total payments) in every jurisdiction where it has been seriously investigated. Even these percentage estimates may be quite low, since only the least sophisticated methods of false ID fraud were uncovered in the investigations. The only characteristic unique to those localities that have reported a significant incidence of false identification fraud in welfare programs is the existence of an investigation of such fraud. We conclude, therefore, that the primary reason for the lack of data on false identification fraud in welfare programs nationwide is that this fraud has been generally unrecognized or ignored.

Periodic audits of federally-sponsored welfare programs by state agencies and the Federal government are required by law. These audits are based on actual cases selected at random and in sufficient numbers to be a statistically valid sample of the total caseload. The audits involve a careful review and investigation of the selected cases. One would suppose, therefore, that these audits would be a fertile and valid source of data on the prevalence of all types of welfare fraud, including false ID fraud. Unfortunately, this is not the case; the audit data is virtually useless in determing the extent of fraud against government. Suspected fraud is not even mentioned in these audits. The objective of the audits according to instructions of the U.S. Department of Health, Education and Welfare (and Department of Agriculture for the food stamp program) is merely to determine "error rates" in the broad categories of ineligibility, overpayment and underpayment. Ineligibility, which means that the audited case should not have received any benefits, could be caused by outright fraud on the part of the recipient or of agency personnel, or simply a procedural error or an innocent mistake. Federal auditors are required to report cases of suspected fraud to state authorities for investigation and possible action; however, the audit reports contain no data on the number of such referrals or any assurance that they are made.

Action to recover public funds from welfare recipients who have committed fraud is the sole responsibility of the state; however, reports of such actions must be made to the Federal government. Those reports show that states which have the highest numbers of ineligible recipients are not necessarily trying to recover the lost funds; in fact, the contrary is true. For example, a recent Federal audit of the food stamp program showed that 50% of the cases audited in Massachusetts were ineligible; this was the highest ineligibility rate in the nation. Yet Massachusetts made no claims against food stamp recipients in fiscal years 1973-1975! In contrast, Utah which had one of the nation's lowest food stamp ineligibility rates at 3.1%, took action in 378 cases over the 1973-1975 period to recover over $103,000 in overpayments from food stamp recipients.

We can only conclude that false identification fraud in welfare programs, like other types of program abuse, is most prevalent where there is the least effort to discover and punish it. We also find that such laxness is encouraged by the failure of Federal agencies to provide effective ID standards for welfare recipients, and failure to enumerate instances of suspected fraud uncovered in audits of state welfare programs and to take action against states which make no effort to deter such abuse.

Social Security Fraud

Social Security programs are responsible for the issuance of over 100 million benefit checks each year, with a total value of $13.7 billion in fiscal 1975. These programs include Retirement and Survivors Insurance (RSI), Disability Income (DI), and Supplemental Security Income (SSI), which provide monthly payments to beneficiaries. An additional $9.2 billion in annual benefits, in the form of reimbursement of medical expenses, is provided under the Health Insurance (HI) program, which includes Medicare. The reported instances of fraud in all these programs has been remarkably low compared to the immense level of payments and number of potential beneficiaries. In 1973, the latest year for which Social Security Administration figures are available, a total of 3,762 potential fraud cases of all types were detected in both RSI and DI programs. Of these cases, 743 or 20% involved falsification of identity, age, or relationship to a covered wage earner, or illegal multiple entitlement. Since documentary evidence must be presented to establish entitlement to benefits, we would classify these as false identification fraud cases. A majority of the suspected fraud cases were cleared following investigation or by agreement to repay the government for any overpayment.

The very low incidence of fraud detected in RSI and DI programs may be explained by several factors. First, coverage under these programs is established by prior payment into the system; in the case of RSI, coverage requires at least 10 years of prior payments. Second, firm documentary evidence and an adjudication period are required to establish entitlement. Third, the Social Security Administration's Bureau of Data Processing has advanced capabilities for record search and retrieval that make successful false ID fraud more difficult.

The SSI program was instituted in 1973 to replace state welfare programs for the elderly, blind and disabled. This program does not require prior payment to establish entitlement, and thus might be somewhat more attractive than the RSI or DI programs to persons intent on fraud. However, no data on the incidence of suspected fraud in the SSI program is yet available.

The largest source of fraud loss in Social Security benefit programs appears to result from the forgery of stolen benefit checks. Social Security checks are stolen more frequently than any other type of check issued by the U.S. Treasury. The probable reason for this fact is that they are regularly mailed to recipients each month. Approximately 47,000 or 65% of the 72,500 forged Treasury checks investigated by the Secret Service during 1975 were Social Security checks. These forgeries of Social Security checks involved a loss to the government of approximately $10 million.

OTHER CRIMINAL ACTIVITY

The foregoing examples illustrate major categories of crimes where the criminal's success is dependent in large measure on the ease with which he can obtain false identification documents; however, the usefulness of false IDs has not been lost on the common criminal engaging in crimes of a lesser scope.

A citizen is most often victimized by the use of false credentials when a criminal tries to gain access to his home, business, or confidence. In large cities, legitimate servicemen and utility company employees often find it difficult to do their job because of the widespread fear of imposters gaining access to homes and apartments using a false ID. Police departments are particularly concerned about the growing use of false police IDs by criminals. Incidents involving police impersonators in New York City totalled 1,358 in 1974, an increase of 88% over 1973, while arrests (268) for this crime increased by only 23% over the same period.

Individuals may also be victimized directly by "confidence men." Investigations conducted in 1974 by the Washington, D.C. Metropolitan Police showed that a false ID was a factor in 50% of the 876 fraud complaints handled. The average fraud complaint involved a loss of about $380.

PART II:
Task Force Reports

TASK FORCE REPORTS

In order to address the many aspects of the use of false identification and to focus the concerns and expertise of its members, the FACFI divided into these five Task Forces:

- Task Force I — Government Payments, which focused on false identification fraud in programs that involve disbursement of monies to individuals by local, state and Federal agencies.

- Task Force II — Commercial Transactions, which was concerned with the fraudulent use of personal identification in over-the-counter sales and bank transactions.

- Task Force III — Fugitives, which concentrated on the use of false identification by fugitives to avoid detection and arrest or linkage to a previous criminal record, to remain in a covert status, or to aid in the commission of further crimes.

- Task Force IV — Federal Documents, which investigated the use of false or fraudulently obtained Federal documents in the conduct of criminal activity.

- Task Force V — State and Local Documents, which focused on the use of false or fraudulently obtained state- and community-issued documents in the commission of crimes.

The initial assignment for each Task Force was to determine the nature and scope of the false identification problem in their area. Task Force reports were to include their findings and preliminary suggestions for solutions. To gather the necessary information, each Task Force examined a variety of public reports and agency records, and conducted seventeen mail surveys of national and international scope. The material gathered in this fashion reflects the experience and the records of several hundred responsible individuals in business, law enforcement, and government.

First drafts of the five Task Force reports were issued between May 1975 and September 1975. The FACFI staff used these reports in developing a summary of the national false identification problem and in formulating preliminary proposals for solutions. The reports from Task Forces I through V have since been redrafted to reduce the amount of repetitive material and to obtain a more uniform and readable format.

REPORT OF THE GOVERNMENT PAYMENTS TASK FORCE

ON THE

SCOPE OF THE FALSE IDENTIFICATION PROBLEM AND

PRELIMINARY RECOMMENDATIONS FOR SOLUTIONS

Submitted to

Federal Advisory Committee On False Identification
David J. Muchow, Chairman

May 1976

CONTENTS

SECTION I — INTRODUCTION 53
    Purpose 53
    Scope 53
    Data Gathering 53
    Evaluation of Data 53

SECTION II — THE FALSE ID PROBLEM 55
    General 55
    Application Phase 55
    Use Phase 56
    Analysis of Programs 56
        Aid to Families with Dependent Children 56
        Medicaid 64
        Food Stamps 64
        Social Security Programs 70

SECTION III — PRELIMINARY RECOMMENDATIONS   75
    General 75
    Recommendations to State Government 75
    Recommendations to Federal Government 77

Report of the Government Payments Task Force

on the

Scope of the False Identification Problem and

Preliminary Recommendations for Solutions

SECTION I

INTRODUCTION

Purpose

The mission of the Task Force is to investigate the national impact of false identification fraud on programs that involve payments by local, state, and federal governments to individuals.

Scope

Four areas, each of which involves programs of national scope, were investigated by the Task Force. These areas included the Aid to Families of Dependent Children (AFDC) and Medicaid programs administered by the Assistance Payments Administration, Department of HEW; the Food Stamp Program of the Department of Agriculture; and four programs administered by the Social Security Administration: Supplemental Security Income (SSI), Health Insurance (HI), Disability Insurance (DI), and Retirement and Survivors Insurance (RSI).

Programs administered by the Veterans Administration and the Department of Housing and Urban Development that involve government payments were not investigated.

Data Gathering

Questionnaires were prepared for each of the four areas investigated. Eighty-six sets of questionnaires covering AFDC, Medicaid and Food Stamps were sent to Directors of Welfare in each state as well as Guam, Puerto Rico and the Virgin Islands; Welfare Quality Control Directors in several states; state and county auditors in several states; and the Inspectors General of New York and Michigan. Twenty sets of questionnaires covering the four Social Security Administration programs were sent to Social Security Headquarters and Regional Offices throughout the country.

Evaluation of Data

Approximately 40% of the questionnaires have been returned. Evident thus far is the apparent lack of information relative to

the frequency of false ID fraud and its fiscal implications. This
lack of information should not be taken to mean that a problem does
not exist. Results of several investigations carried out independently by individual states and localities will be cited that show
significant impact from false ID fraud in government payments programs. Several of the returned questionnaires have contained
expressions of deep concern about the use of false identification
and the hope that something can be done to alleviate the problem.
The Office of the Commissioner of Welfare, Department of HEW, has
recommended on several occasions to the National Welfare Fraud
Association that information on frequency and impact of false ID
fraud should be collected by the states and reported to the NEW
National Center of Social Statistics in Washington, D.C.

SECTION II

THE FALSE ID PROBLEM

General

False ID fraud in government-assisted welfare and social insurance programs has significant national problem potential because of the ubiquitous nature and staggering dollar volume of such programs. For example, in January 1975, a nationwide average of 11.1 million AFDC recipients were receiving benefits at the rate of $730 million each month; this represents an annual cost to taxpayers of $8.8 billion. The federal government issued over 100 million benefit checks in fiscal 1975 under SSI, DI, and RSI programs; these checks represented a total dollar value of over $13.7 billion. Benefits under the HI program (which includes Medicare) amounted to an additional $9.2 billion in fiscal 1975.

Government payments programs have generally displayed a steady growth in beneficiaries over recent years; the growth of some programs, such as Food Stamps, has been spectacular. In 1965, recipients of Food Stamp benefits numbered 400,000 and total benefits were $36 million. As of January 1975, the program had expanded over a hundredfold to encompass 19.1 million recipients and a payment level of $5.2 billion per year. Programs of this scale present many opportunities for abuse by fraud, whether by false ID or not. Even if only a small percentage of the transactions between government and the beneficiaries of these programs are fraudulent, the total dollar loss to taxpayers in direct payments and costs of fraud detection and prosecution can be very high. Thus, although our surveys have indicated that false ID fraud is generally viewed as only a small part of total program abuse, the Government Payments Task Force has concluded that such fraud constitutes a significant national problem that is deserving of further study.

Government payment programs are subjected to false ID fraud in both "application" and "use" phases of the programs and these are discussed below.

Application Phase

All the programs studied by the Task Force require some sort of application for future benefits. During this "application phase," applicants are asked to identify themselves and any dependents on whose behalf program benefits are sought. The types of identification documents currently required by state agencies were found to vary widely, ranging from none at all to a self-consistent set of official documents. The most commonly used documents in false ID fraud in this phase appear to be birth and baptismal certificates, state-issued driver's licenses, and Social Security cards.

Fraudulent documents are obtained in a number of ways. Birth certificates are usually genuine documents that have been altered and then photocopied. Baptismal and some birth certificates, on the other hand, can be easily generated by forging data on official appearing blanks bought at stationery stores or through mail order companies. Fraudulently used driver's licenses are obtained through theft and counterfeiting; they can also be obtained by application, using a false birth certificate as a "breeder" document. Although the Social Security card was never intended to be used as an identity document, it is used extensively as such in both legitimate and fraudulent transactions. Until recently, little identification was required to establish a new Social Security account. Thus, it was possible for an individual to establish accounts under several aliases. This has led to the collection of multiple benefits not only from Social Security programs but also from other government payments programs in which the multiple Social Security cards served as "identity documents" at application. Social Security cards have also been obtained by theft or counterfeiting. Unofficial "permanent" Social Security cards made of metal can also be obtained by supplying mail-order firms with an account number that is assumed or fictitious; these unofficial cards are sometimes used successfully for identification.

The period between application for government benefits and the receipt of benefits varies from a few days (or weeks) in the case of emergency relief payments to several months (or years) in the case of certain Social Security programs.

Use Phase

False ID has been employed in the "use" phase when persons fraudulently assume the identity of others to collect their benefits. This use of false ID occurs most commonly in the cashing of stolen government checks or Food Stamps. Apparently, many banks and businesses are willing to cash these instruments without adequate identification of the endorser.

Analysis of Programs

The following sections present analyses by the Task Force of surveys of AFDC, Medicaid, Food Stamp, and Social Security programs. The analyses describe the range of requirements for recipient identification in application and use phases of the programs, and give available data on the scope of the false identification problem.

Aid to Families with Dependent Children

Sources of Information

Twenty-eight responses to the questionnaires on the use of false identification to obtain Aid to Families with Dependent Children (AFDC) have been received. Respondents represent twenty-five states, one county (Los Angeles), one territory (Guam), and the Commonwealth of Puerto Rico.

The Normal Process

The AFDC process begins when an applicant (generally one adult and one or more children) indicates verbally or in writing that they are in need of public assistance. Initial application may be made by phone, in writing or by personal appearance at a local political subdivision. Eligibility for public assistance under the AFDC program is limited to U.S. citizens and legal aliens permanently residing in the U.S. Eligibility criteria include resource and income limitations, financial need and deprivation. When application is made and the welfare organization is satisfied that the applicant is indeed eligible, instructions are generally forwarded to an office of the state welfare organization from which grants are issued. In some states, grants are prepared centrally within counties, in others by the state welfare office and still others by the state controller or treasurer.

Once AFDC eligibility is established, states are not required to issue an AFDC identification document to recipients. Of the twenty-eight respondents to the questionnaire, 5 issue a photo ID, 2 issue an ID with no photo and 21 issue no ID at all.

The financial assistance provided to AFDC recipients is usually in the form of a semi-monthly check or warrant. Nationwide, as of January 1975, there were an average of 11.1 million AFDC recipients receiving benefits each month.

ID for Benefits

It is evident that a wide variety of documents are acceptable for the initial identification of AFDC applicants. The types of documents accepted and the number of respondents accepting them follow:

1. Birth Certificate..........................22
2. Social Security Card......................16
3. Drivers License...........................14
4. Welfare ID (if former recipient)........... 7
5. Credit Cards.............................. 6
6. Employer Identification Card..............10
7. Selective Service Card....................10
8. Military Identification Card..............10
9. Military Discharge Papers.................13
10. Food Stamp ID............................ 8
11. Union ID Card............................ 8

     12. Immigration and Naturalization Documents...17
     13. Baptismal Records.......................... 5
     14. Marriage Certificates...................... 4

   Of interest is the fact that five states returning questionnaires make no attempt to verify an applicant's identity. Some states only require identification to verify the birth of the children for whom assistance is sought, but none for the adult applicant who will also receive assistance. Most jurisdictions rarely, if ever, check the authenticity of "breeder" identification documents.

   The importance of an effective identification program is illustrated by a report[1] of the Office of the New York State Comptroller.

   The New York Legislature, according to this report, mandated that the New York City Human Resources Administration issue photo identification cards to all recipients of public assistance in the AFDC program. "The primary purpose of the Photo ID was to (reduce or) prevent the cashing of lost and stolen checks."

   This report found that "as of May, 1973, about 3,000 cases were closed as a result of the Photo ID program. This represented a savings of about $7.2 million a year in payments to ineligible recipients."[1] This reduction in caseload apparently came about either as the result of fictitious cases being closed or an "unwillingness" to be photographed on the part of some recipients.

ID for Check Cashing

   The types of documents accepted as a means of identifying recipients when benefits are obtained (e.g., when AFDC checks are cashed), depends on the criteria established by the banks and merchants who cash the checks. Unfortunately, a significant number of banks and merchants require little if any identification when cashing government checks. Checks are cashed under the false assumption that government issued checks are automatically "good." Evidence of this can be seen in Figure 1, a chart prepared by the Department of the Treasury, Fiscal Service, Operations Planning and Research Staff in a study entitled "Report on Forged Treasury Checks."

   The basis of the Treasury report was a review of all forged checks for which a formal affidavit of forgery was filed with the Treasurer of the United States during the month of August, 1972.

---

[1] Audit Report on Photo ID Program, New York City Human Resources Administration, Report No. NYC-22-74, Feb. 15, 1974.

[1] Emphasis added.

ENDORSER'S IDENTIFICATION

Financial/ Commercial Establishment Where Cashed	Driver's License No.	Driver's License % of Col. 7	Social Security No.	Social Security % of Col. 7	Regiscope Picture No.	Regiscope Picture % of Col. 7	Employment I.D. No.	Employment I.D. % of Col. 7	Check Cashing Card No.	Check Cashing Card % of Col. 7	All Other Forms [1] No.	All Other Forms [1] % of Col. 7	Total I.D. Forms [2] No.	Total I.D. Forms [2] % of Total in this Col.	Items Showing I.D. No.	Items Showing I.D. % of Col. 10	Items Not Showing I.D. No.	Items Not Showing I.D. % of Col. 10	Total Items No.	Total Items % of Total
	(1)		(2)		(3)		(4)		(5)		(6)		(7)		(8)		(9)		(10)	
Commercial Bank	49	18.6	31	11.7	12	4.6	22	8.3	24	9.1	126	47.7	264	30.8	231	19.1	979	80.9	1210	30.4
Grocery Store	17	14.3	17	14.3	29	24.4	3	2.5	10	8.4	43	36.1	119	13.9	99	15.9	522	84.1	621	15.6
Liquor Store	5	20.8	3	12.5	6	25.0	1	4.2	—	—	9	37.5	24	2.8	22	13.5	141	86.5	163	4.1
Check-Cashing Firm	1	5.6	—	—	12	66.6	—	—	1	5.6	4	22.2	18	2.1	18	16.5	91	83.5	109	2.8
Department Store	14	28.6	8	16.3	2	4.1	6	12.2	2	4.1	17	34.7	49	5.7	38	32.8	78	67.2	116	2.9
Other Estbmt. [3]	6	33.3	4	22.2	2	11.1	1	—	—	—	6	33.3	18	2.1	18	8.6	192	91.4	210	5.3
All Others	17	16.3	14	13.5	14	13.5	8	7.7	2	1.9	49	47.1	104	12.2	92	13.6	585	86.4	677	17.0
Total Legible Items	109	18.2	77	12.9	77	12.9	40	6.7	39	6.6	254	42.6	596	69.6	518	16.7	2588	83.3	3106	78.1
Items Not Legible	44	16.9	20	7.7	10	3.8	13	5.0	1	.4	172	66.2	260	30.4	224	25.7	648	74.3	872	21.9
Total Items	153	17.9	97	11.4	87	10.2	53	6.2	40	4.7	426	49.8	856	100.0	742	18.7	3236	81.3	3978	100.0%

[1] Covers all other forms of I.D. presented, including principally military I.D. (32), Credit Cards (17), fingerprints (7), voter card I.D. (7).
[2] The total number of I.D. forms presented is greater than the number of items bearing I.D. information because in 114 cases two forms of I.D. were shown on one item.
[3] Covers six other types of establishments, each cashing more than ten checks, as follows: Gasoline Stations (55), Drug Stores (54), Bar (44), Savings & Loan Associations (36), Realty Firm/Housing Authority (11), and Nursing Home (10).

Figure 1 — Establishment Where Checks Cashed Relative to Identification Shown

A total of 3,978 forged instruments were reviewed. The chart, comparing the types of identification used with the establishments accepting them, reveals that 81.3% or 3,236 forged checks did not contain written evidence on the check that an ID was used at the time of cashing. The study found that "the rate of acceptance of drivers' licenses and Social Security cards as a means of identification is particularly high in department stores and other establishments whereas these identification forms (except for one instance) are unacceptable to check-cashing firms. Also, use of the Regiscope[3] as a means of identification is relatively low in commercial banks (4.6%) and department stores (4.1%), relatively high in grocery (24.4%) and liquor (25%) stores, and extremely high in check-cashing firms (66.6%)."

AFDC Fraud

The survey requested specific information on the extent and impact of AFDC identification-related fraud. Data requested included the number of fraud cases investigated in which false ID was used, the fiscal impact of the fraud, estimates of the percentage of total AFDC frauds that involve false ID, administrative costs of prosecuting false ID, and types and use of false ID encountered.

Twenty-three of twenty-eight responses to all these queries left the questions blank or stated that the information was either not available or unknown. The states supplying some of the requested information estimated that less than 2% of AFDC fraud cases involved the use of false identification. However, one state readily admitted that because fraud reports do not generally specify the nature of the fraud, true percentages are likely to be much higher. As a result, the Task Force has concluded that the frequency of the use of false identification remains undetermined because of the lack of adequate information at all levels of government and the private sector.

Because of the dearth of information, it is necessary to turn to specific welfare fraud reports in order to demonstrate the seriousness of the false identification problem. It should be pointed out that the available reports are not limited to obvious problems of false identification, but include numerous other fraudulent practices such as forgery, which is a false ID crime, the check itself being the false ID. It is abundantly clear that if proper identification is required at the time a public assistance check is cashed, millions of dollars can be saved annually.

The Mail Theft Issue

One of the most serious problems encountered by jurisdictions that mail checks to welfare recipients is mail theft. A Pennsylvania

---

[3] A device that photographs both the check and the individual cashing the check.

study[1] has found that "Pennsylvania welfare checks are stolen with much greater frequency" than any other checks sent by mail. A prime reason for this is due to the length of time it takes Pennsylvania to complete an investigation on reports of lost or stolen checks. In September and October, 1974, it was found that investigations of non-receipt complaints currently in progress in the Philadelphia area were for "checks issued in July of 1971." It should be noted that similar delays are common in many of the larger metropolitan areas throughout the country.

Most states, including Pennsylvania, upon receiving a report of a lost or stolen check, have the recipient complete an affidavit and issue a replacement check within twenty-four or forty-eight hours. These affidavits are used as the basis for collecting information to be used in any subsequent investigation. The Pennsylvania Grand Jury found that the majority of non-receipt claims cannot be resolved after a search of the files of the State Treasury Department. Statistics indicate that "approximately 41% of the cases are determined to involve checks that have been stolen or forged." Another 20% of the cases are determined to constitute fraud, that is, a check was received and cashed by the welfare recipient but subsequently reported as lost or stolen, in order to obtain a double payment. A study by the New York State Comptroller[1] found that over thirty percent of the checks for which replacements have been issued are subsequently determined to have been fraudulently cashed.

These percentages are shocking when one considers the number of replacement checks issued. The Pennsylvania Federal Grand Jury found the following:

"For the month of January, 1971, the incredible total of over twenty-six thousand replacement checks was issued in Philadelphia alone. Since the average welfare check amounts to approximately one hundred and eight dollars, the value of these replacement checks was more than two million six hundred thousand dollars. In 1972 and early 1973, ten thousand replacement checks, totalling over one million dollars, were being issued each month in Philadelphia alone. That figure is currently reduced to four or five thousand replacement checks per month, with an approximate value of one-half million dollars. This reduction, however, should not lull us into

---

[1] Report of the Federal Grand Jury for the Eastern District of Pennsylvania on Welfare Check Theft and Fraud in Pennsylvania and the Administrative Processing of Pennsylvania Welfare Recipient Complaints on Non-Receipt.

[1] Audit Report on Fraudulent Duplicate Check Claims, New York City Human Resources Administration, NYC-50-74.

believing that there has been a proportionately great reduction in the rate of theft of welfare checks. The continued and diversified enforcement efforts of the Postal Inspectors and some improvements in the processing of these checks have reduced the theft rate. However, most of the reduction of monthly replacement checks from twenty-six thousand to five thousand is the result of a substantial reduction in the number of checks being delivered by the mails."

The Fraudulent Deplicate Check Claims audit in New York City revealed that in fiscal year 1974, the City's public assistance payments were approximately $1.2 billion. The audit found that "during the year ended October, 1973, HRA (Human Resources Administration of New York City) replaced 310,000 checks worth $28 million which had been reported lost or stolen." They also found that "as of November, 1973, there was a backlog of 110,000 fraudulently cashed checks worth $9.7 million on which no recoupment action had been taken."

These figures are substantiated by the Report on Investigation of Welfare Fraud by Office of the Queens District Attorney for the Year 1974. This report states that "the most serious problem faced in the administration of Public Assistance and one for which there are no adequate present safeguards is the multiple collection of welfare payments by people using several aliases." The report further states that "it appears that the only way to eliminate this type of welfare cheating is to require a form of identification which is absolutely unique to each individual and which is not capable of fraudulent duplication."

A recent article in the Washington Post on check thieves and their victims, with emphasis on federally issued checks, indicates that upwards of $15,000,000 are lost due to forgery. The article stated:

"The check thieves steal about $50,000 a day by forging government checks. Most of those direct losses are carried by the banks and businesses that cash the forged checks. The indirect costs borne by various government departments that investigate and replace the stolen checks runs into the millions each year."

A recent review conducted by the New York State Office of Audit and Quality Control showed that welfare checks issued by the State of New York alone account for $12,000,000 in fraudulently cashed checks each year. It is likely that if similar studies were made of fraudulently cashed government checks issued in other major metropolitan areas across the county, these figures would double or triple. It is unlikely that the New York and Philadelphia metropolitan areas are the only ones experiencing these problems.

False ID Suspect Profile

The most common characteristics of individuals who have come under investigation for using fraudulent identification in order to obtain AFDC benefits are as follows:

1. 20-30 years of age;
2. Female;
3. Unemployed;
4. Has completed 12 years of education;
5. Resides in a metropolitan area;
6. The fraud occurred in a metropolitan area;
7. Had no prior criminal record; and
8. Has resided in present residence six months.

Apparent thus far is the fact that the amount of detectable fraud is commensurate with the effort made to detect it. As an example, of 343 cases sent to the prosecutor by the Special Investigative Section of the Department of Social and Health Services in the State of Washington, 338 or 98.5% resulted in guilty verdicts. This occurred in the first year of their operation beginning August, 1973. The annual report of the Special Investigation Unit for Suffolk County, New York, stated that "as a result of activities by the Special Investigation Unit in the year 1974, over one million dollars in fraud was uncovered, and resulted in an additional savings to the County of $900,000 in Public Assistance cases being closed."

The Treasury Department[1] expresses the frustration of those in government concerned with the fraudulent cashing of checks and the question of proper identification. They state:

"It is apparent that check-cashing establishments, and particularly banks, do not take proper precautions. They are accepting checks (in some cases for large dollar amounts) with questionable endorsements and forms of identification which are not, obviously, reliable. It is entirely conceivable that strict observance of the simple maxim 'Know your endorser - require identification' would reduce substantially the incidence of encashment of stolen and forged Treasury checks."

---

[1] "Report on Forged Treasury Checks," Department of the Treasury, Fiscal Service Operations Planning and Research Staff.

Medicaid

Sources of Information

Twenty-six responses to the questionnaires on the use of false identification to obtain Medicaid benefits have been received by respondents representing twenty-four states, one county (Los Angeles) and one territory (Guam).

Analysis of Data Received

While all states issue some form of Medicaid identification card and/or Medicaid labels, the conclusion that must be drawn from the responses received is that states have little, if any, knowledge concerning the use of false identification in the Medicaid program. A common response is that states are "not required" to keep Medicaid fraud statistics and, therefore, do not.

The states that did provide some information indicate that the problem appears to be more in the nature of provider fraud rather than recipient fraud. One state that found some recipients using Medicaid cards belonging to other persons discovered that in most instances the imposters were themselves eligible for Medicaid or other medical assistance but had lost or mislaid their own Medicaid ID.

The Task Force is, therefore, unable to provide any meaningful data relative to the use of false identification in obtaining Medicaid benefits.

The Task Force believes that states should be required to maintain uniform and detailed statistics on Medicaid fraud. In addition to providing meaningful national data, such statistics would serve as administrative tools for corrective action at all government levels.

Food Stamps

Sources of Information

The Food Stamp questionnaire was mailed to Welfare Departments of all U.S. states and territories. Twenty-four responses have been received; respondents represent twenty-two states, one county (Los Angeles), and one territory (Guam). Maryland's response consisted of twelve separate questionnaires filled out by officials of as many counties.

The Normal Process

The Food Stamp application process begins when an individual or family applies for benefits at a local or state welfare office (in many urban areas, community service organizations serve under

contract to the state as registration offices). Eligibility for
Food Stamp benefits is limited to U.S. citizens and legal aliens
in permanent residence and is based on income level, number of
dependents, and certain other eligibility requirements. Recipients
of federally-supported state assistance programs such as Aid to
Families with Dependent Children (AFDC) are automatically eligible
for Food Stamp benefits. If the local registration office is
satisfied that the applicant meets eligibility criteria, the
application is forwarded to an office of the state welfare department for a final determination. Upon a favorable determination,
the applicant is provided with a Food Stamp ID card and (in most
states) his first Authorization to Purchase (ATP) card. The Food
Stamp ID is usually not a photo ID card; in Massachusetts, for
example, it is a machine-readable card containing the applicant's
name, Social Security Number, and signature. The name and signature of an authorized proxy may also appear on the card. The
ATP document is also a machine-readable card containing the
authorized face value of food coupons to be purchased and the
purchase price. The purchase price is determined by the need of
the applicant and ranges from zero to slightly less than the face
value of the coupons. Food Stamps may be purchased at state-
authorized outlets, which are usually banks but may be retail
stores or community service agencies. The "stamps" (more properly
coupons) are issued by the federal government. ATP are presently
issued monthly; revalidation, which entails redetermination of
eligibility and issuance of a new Food Stamp ID, is required every
three months.

ID at Registration

It is apparent that there is no nationally-accepted standard
for identification of Food Stamp applicants upon registration.
Eight states require no identity documents at this point. Fourteen
of the twenty-six respondents accept a Social Security card as
identification at registration; nine accept a driver's license,
and eleven accept immigration and naturalization documents. Several
respondents noted "if applicable" on immigration documents, imply-
ing that selection was exercised in demanding proof of citizenship.
One respondent (a Southwestern state) indicated that ID was required
"only if citizenship is questioned." All the documents suggested
as choices[1] are accepted by at least three of the respondents.
Other documents not listed but accepted by one or more respondents
include library cards, income documents, bills, and "personal
papers." Some of the respondents indicated that the responsibility
of the state agencies is to determine the eligibility and need level
of the applicant, not his true identity.

---

[1] The list of suggested documents appears in the description of AFDC
programs in this report; current and expired Food Stamp ID's were
added to this list.

ID for Claiming Stamps

The standards for identification of recipients picking up Food Stamps in person are apparently tighter and more uniform than those applying at registration. Twenty-three of the twenty-six respondents accept a current Food Stamp ID at this point; several respondents accept only this document for Food Stamp pickup. Ten respondents would accept the Food Stamp ID of a former recipient, six a driver's license, and five a current welfare ID. Only one respondent indicated that most of the documents listed as choices[2] are accepted; none indicated that no ID is required for Food Stamp pickup.

ID for Food Purchase

The Food Stamp ID was also most frequently mentioned (nineteen responses) as the usual document required when Food Stamps are used to purchase food. Nine respondents indicated that an old Food Stamp ID would be accepted. Four respondents stated that the required ID would depend on the "sales outlet" at which the stamps were used, while two believed that no ID is usually required by food stores.

Food Stamp Fraud

Specific information was requested to the extent and impact of Food Stamp Fraud. The number of fraud cases investigated in which false ID was used, the fiscal impact of the fraud, estimates of the fraction of total Food Stamp frauds that involve false ID, administrative costs of prosecuting false ID, and types and use of false ID encountered. Unfortunately, the most common response (ten of twenty-six) to all these queries was "Information Not Available." One respondent's comment summarized the apparent attitude of many state welfare departments: "No record kept (of this type of information) since there is no requirement to do so." Almost as common (nine responses) was the comment that false ID fraud is nonexistent in the respondent's jurisdiction[1]. This was not only the response of such sparsely populated rural states as Oklahoma, North Dakota, and Montana, but also of urban states such as Connecticut and Delaware.

Completely in contrast to these responses was the report submitted by the State of Arkansas. This report covered only Non-Public Assistance Food Stamp recipients in North Pulaski County, which includes only 2.5% of statewide Food Stamp recipients. Nevertheless, in FY 73-74, this county (which includes part of Little Rock, Ark.) recorded 57 cases of false ID fraud carrying a loss to the Federal government of $18,740. All cited cases involved

---

[2] Same as suggested for Food Stamp application.

[1] If no records are maintained, it is questionable as to whether such a statement can be given much credence.

false ID at the time of application; seven cases also included the use of false ID at the time of food purchase. In 31 cases, imposter identification was used; counterfeit identification was used in 24 cases; and altered identification in 2 cases. The state estimated its administrative cost in prosecuting these cases to be $3500.

The Arkansas data are extremely significant, considering the relatively small sample of Food Stamp recipients that yielded all these cases. Two possible explanations of the data are suggested: either Little Rock, Ark. is a hotbed of false ID fraud, or the problem is being overlooked (and therefore declared nonexistent) in most of the nation. Some additional information, quoted from the Arkansas response, suggests that the latter explanation is more nearly correct:

> "Since April 1974, the prosecuting attorney in Pulaski County has been extremely concerned with all aspects of recipient abuse of the Food Stamp Program and has been very active in the prosecution of food stamp fraud cases. To date, three hundred and ten (310) felony charges of false pretense have been filed against one hundred and twenty-seven (127) persons in Pulaski County. Thus far eleven (11) persons have been found guilty with sentencing ranging from five (5) years in the State Penitentiary to one (1) year suspended."

Substantive data on false ID fraud was also received from Los Angeles County, California. However, no special breakout for Food Stamp fraud could be provided: the figures given refer to welfare fraud of all types. False ID fraud cases investigated increased from 24 in FY 70-71 to 103 in FY 73-74. Estimated welfare and Food Stamp payments to recipients as a result of this fraud totalled $24,170 in FY 70-71 and $85,148 in FY 73-74.

Common ID Fraud Documents

The documents most frequently used in false ID fraud in Arkansas are Social Security Cards and Food Stamp ID documents. Social Security Cards are obtained by application under one or more false names; unofficial "permanent" Social Security cards made of aluminum are obtained by mail order and sometimes used as ID documents. The most frequent abuse of the non-photographic Food Stamp ID is the "loan" of it to unauthorized parties who then use it in purchasing Food Stamps. Apparently, the intermediate ATP document is not used in Arkansas.

California listed baptismal and birth certificates and driver's licenses as the most frequently abused ID documents. Birth certificates are commonly used to support the existence and ages of claimed dependent children; blank baptismal certificates are available in stationery stores, while birth certificates are most frequently genuine documents that are altered and then photocopied.

Most of the driver's licenses used in false ID fraud in California were counterfeit documents.

False ID Suspect Profile

Arkansas and California showed good agreement in their profile of the typical suspect in false ID investigation; both identified a young (18-30) unemployed woman resident in a metropolitan area. California described the typical suspect as not having a prior criminal record, while Arkansas could not supply data on prior criminal records. Both states cited metropolitan areas as the most common locales for ID fraud.

Extent of the Problem

None of the twenty-six respondents to the Food Stamp survey indicated a belief that false ID fraud represents a majority of total Food Stamp fraud cases. However, the Arkansas response, which contained the most detailed data on false ID fraud, estimated the proportion of false ID cases as 10% of the total fraud cases. Much more common methods of fraud include falsification of income, medical expenses, or number of dependents. In Los Angeles County, the percentage of welfare fraud cases investigated that involved false ID was less than 1% for all years reported (FY 70-74 inclusive). Estimates of false ID fraud as percentages of total Food Stamp fraud supplied by other respondents ranged from below 1% to 5%; no basis for these estimates was given.

Analysis of ID Fraud Data

These estimates establish clearly that the use of false ID is perceived as a minor problem with respect to overall abuse of the Food Stamp program. Three comments, however, appear to be in order. They are: (1) Based on the wide variance of the Arkansas response from the national sample, <u>false ID fraud is probably much more widespread and considerably more frequent than most state welfare departments realize</u>; (2) <u>All of the methods of false ID use that were detected are very primitive</u>. This includes the unauthorized use of Food Stamp ID, phony or duplicate Social Security Cards, and counterfeit driver's licenses; and (3) More sophisticated methods of false ID (such as Infant Death Identity)[1] could be in widespread use but not currently detected.

Disposition of Cases

Cases of Food Stamp fraud, when discovered, are referred to the local prosecutor's office (usually county-level) for disposition. The cost-sharing provisions of the Food Stamp program do not provide a strong incentive for state and local prosecution of Food Stamp fraud; in fact, they provide the states with a strong

---

[1] See Part I, Section 3 of the FACFI Final Report.

disincentive. The states pay a portion of the administrative costs of the program, including costs for the apprehension and prosecution of offenders. The entire cost of the coupons fraudulently obtained, on the other hand, is borne by the Federal government. Therefore, added emphasis on fraud results in <u>added costs to the state, yet all funds recovered must be returned to the Federal government</u>. Stolen or forged Food Stamp ID and ATP cards can be used at banks and retail stores to obtain and "spend" coupons where no effort is made to confirm the identity of the bearer. The Food Stamp ID used in most states is not a photo ID and can, in certain cases, be used by a proxy to purchase coupons for a designated recipient. These characteristics make it relatively easy to counterfeit or to use if stolen. Federal guidelines for state action (FNS [FS] Instruction 736-1) make it extremely unlikely that states will elect to prosecute any but the most flagrant abusers of the Food Stamp program. Finally, several respondents to the Food Stamp survey indicated that communication is poor between state and local welfare officials regarding abuses of the Food Stamp program.

Suggestions for Solutions

Several suggestions were made by survey respondents to consider the problem of false ID fraud. Establishment of a photo ID system was the most common suggestion. One respondent, however, in making this suggestion noted that this "would be one more harassment to Food Stamp Program participants." One state suggested that others follow its practice of mailing Food Stamp ID and ATP documents in separate envelopes; this makes it more difficult for a thief to obtain both documents. One respondent preferred the (apparently older) FS-4 form to the ATP card "since the former permits close control over currency of ID." The Arkansas respondent suggested requiring more than one form of ID at intake to the program. Finally, one respondent appealed to the Federal government to "simplify program specification to free workers to perform other tasks, such as checking ID!"

An overall view of the responses suggests the need for some uniform type of identification requirement to be used at application. Application frauds using counterfeit or imposter identities appear to be the most common types of known ID fraud. The Social Security card was mentioned most frequently as a document used in false ID fraud; until recently it has been very easy to obtain Social Security cards under assumed identities. It remains to be seen whether new regulations by the Social Security Administration will have a long-range effect on the false ID problem. For the present, acceptance of the Social Security card alone as an ID for the Food Stamp program should certainly be discouraged. More fundamentally, there is a need to restructure the balance of state and Federal responsibilities in the Food Stamp program to improve the efficiency of its administration and to discourage abuses of the program.

Social Security Programs

Sources of Information

The Social Security questionnaire was sent to appropriate Social Security Administration bureaus, including those responsible for Supplemental Security Income (SSI), Health Insurance (HI), Disability Insurance (DI), and Retirement and Survivors Insurance (RSI). In addition, copies were sent to the Division of International Operations (RSI) and the Documents Analysis Laboratory in the Office of Administration, a rich source of information. It was the opinion of the Laboratory Chief that "false identification" is a very small part of the false documentation problem at the Social Security Administration.

The Normal Process

Social Security programs are unique among those considered by the Government Payments Task Force in that a large majority of the working population of the U.S. is registered for benefits under these programs. Registration or opening of a Social Security Account typically takes place upon an individual's first application for salary or wage paying work. Prior to 1974, little or no documentary evidence of identity was required to register for Social Security benefits. There is some evidence of multiple registrations under a variety of aliases, a procedure which can enable the collection of multiple benefits. The Social Security Administration instituted procedures in 1974 calling for presentation of documentary evidence of identity upon registration.

Once registered, an individual in covered employment is subject to withholding of Social Security contributions; similar contributions are required of employers. Federal law requires that any change affecting contributions to the program, such as marriage and acquisition or loss of dependents, be reported promptly to the Social Security Administration.

Application for benefits, as distinct from registration, normally occurs when an individual enters a status eligible for benefits. Eligible circumstances include retirement after age 62, permanent disability, blindness, and for survivors, the death of a covered wage earner. Documentary evidence of eligibility must be presented with the application for benefits. However, no investigation of the claim is usually made unless there is some reason for suspicion. Referrals of possible fraud in Social Security cases generally originate from voluntary informants.

ID Required

Only the birth certificate and Social Security card were listed by all components as being accepted for initial determination for eligibility. The Supplemental Security Income Program appears to accept more types of documents initially than any other bureau of the Social Security Administration.

The types of documents shown as an acceptable means of identifying recipients when benefits are obtained, either when checks are cashed or services received, are varied. All four bureaus indicated that documents such as driver licenses, marriage certificates, credit cards, etc., are used. In fact, only two types of identification mentioned on the questionnaire that were not used by any bureau were the Welfare ID and the Food Stamp ID. From these statistics, it appears that the most common document used for identification purposes is the driver's license which is easily obtained, altered, and forged. Another in common use is the Social Security card which was never intended to be used for identification purposes.

Social Security Program Fraud

The most common response to fraud impact question was "information not available." The survey yielded a total of only 56 cases investigated for fraud in the four fiscal years 1970-1974 that involved the use of false identity. Of these, 17 cases were classified as altered ID, 5 as counterfeits, and 21 as imposter cases; classification was not made for the other 8 cases. No records of fraud based on false identity have been kept by the Disability Insurance Bureau.

In response to Question F, number of cases in which applicants for benefits were refused benefits because they could or would not provide identification, the Bureau of Health Insurance stated that in their program, services could conceivably be performed in emergency situations even if an individual did not have his health insurance identification card. They pointed out, though, that the physician or provider may not be able to collect from Medicare if it develops that the patient was not entitled to the services performed. All other respondents indicated that they were not aware of any cases.

It was generally agreed among the respondents that it cannot be assumed that if identification is required, fraud has not taken place. In most cases, if a person decides to file a false application he would also have obtained false identification. In addition, it is not always possible to detect the fraudulent act unless a complete and extensive investigation is initiated when the claim is filed. In many cases, the fraudulent act is detected by reports from informers or through development of the initial claim, a subsequent claim, or a post adjudicative discrepancy.

Relative to administrative costs and manpower resources for fraud investigation involving false identification, it appears that only a very small percentage of time is spent on the problem of false identification. In fact, 5 percent or less of all cases examined for possible fraud by the Document Analysis Laboratory at the Social Security Administration involve false identification. These cases usually do not involve attempts at false identity. Rather, the individual has attempted to change certain facts about himself for personal benefit. For example, he may attempt to show that he is older than he actually is in order to qualify for retirement benefits.

False ID Techniques

The most common techniques for obtaining fraudulent identification as reported were:

1. File several Forms SS-5 (Application for a Social Security Account Number) using completely different identifying information on each application (i.e., different name, parent's names, place of birth, birth date). When application is made on the various account numbers, a false birth certificate or affidavit supposedly signed by the parent is used;

2. Find or steal another person's Social Security card;

3. Applicant, who may be receiving wife's or widow's benefits, can file for retirement insurance using maiden name and falsely state that she had not previously filed for benefits;

4. An applicant can obtain the birth certificate of a person who died at an early age and then proceed to use that individual's identity to build up another wage record and subsequently file under the new account number;

5. An applicant can assume the identity of a wage earner's legal wife, with the wage earner's knowledge, using the marriage record pertaining to the legal wife as proof of age on the basis of her allegation that this was the only proof of age available;

6. Contact a church and obtain a baptismal certificate of an individual who is not the requester of said certificate;

7. Obtain fraudulent documents from outside the United States from both civil and religious sources, such as local civil registries and church records. It is sometimes possible to bribe the civil or church official to issue fraudulent documents.

False ID Suspect Profile

There was general agreement among all respondents as to the profile of the typical suspect in false ID investigation: most are at least 65, can be either male or female, many are unemployed, with little known regarding their educational backgrounds. There are more cases of attempted use of false identification in metropolitan areas than rural or suburban areas, possibly because little or no identification is required in less populated areas since people tend to know each other better.

Control of Abuse

It is a Federal offense subject to criminal penalties for an individual to furnish false information to the Social Security Administration in connection with the establishment and maintenance of Social Security earnings records, to use a Social Security number (SSN) with false information, to use a counterfeit SSN, or to use someone else's SSN.

There are definite procedures to follow when a beneficiary fails to receive a check. Briefly, a beneficiary reports the nonreceipt to the SSA district office which in turn will forward the nonreceipt allegation to the Treasury Disbursing Center which has responsibility for issuing the payment. At this point, a request is made to place a stop payment in the Treasury system against the original check. If the original check is later presented for payment, the Treasury will make the determination as to the proper method of recovery. When a nonreceipt claim is received and the original check is paid by the Treasury and the check is found to bear an unauthorized endorsement, the Department of the Treasury will request directly the refund of these payments.

Suggestions for Solutions

Several suggestions were made to counter the problem of false ID fraud. The use of the Social Security numbers as a universal identifier was the most common suggestion. However, this has already been considered in terms of the danger of invasion of privacy, the cost to the Federal Government, the time required to institute the system and the effectiveness of such a system for alleviating the problem. The use of the number for such a system seems unlikely at this time. Other respondents suggested that more specific care should be taken in identifying the claimant. They further suggested that all documentary proofs should be examined carefully. If any document appears altered or not authentic, a Document Specialist should be requested to verify the document. When fraud is suspected, development of the fraud aspects should be started quickly. Another suggestion was the universal use of one or more corroborating documents, rather than the use of only one. Along these lines, an applicant for a Social Security number must show convincing evidence of identity. Preferably, the evidence will show his age or date of birth, his address, and his signature, and be at least several months old. Still another common suggestion was that all individuals applying for Social Security numbers could be fingerprinted when applying for benefits in order to establish their identity. This too would probably be unfeasible and not readily accepted by the public.

SECTION III

PRELIMINARY RECOMMENDATIONS

General

    The Government Payments Task Force presents in this section a list of preliminary recommendations to reduce the incidence of false ID fraud in the programs studied. These recommendations were developed from survey responses, by individual Task Force members after a review of survey findings, and by other individuals with whom Task Force members had contact. It should be emphasized that these recommendations represent individual viewpoints and do not necessarily reflect the opinions of all Task Force members. The recommendations have also not yet been screened, compared, and examined with respect to such criteria as cost effectiveness, practicality, and likelihood of public acceptance. Since detailed management of cost-shared welfare programs, including AFDC, Medicaid, and Food Stamps, is relegated to individual states, while Social Security is a strictly Federal program, recommendations have been divided into those that apply to state and Federal governments.

Recommendations to State Government

1. Provide a tamper-proof identification card which may be used for all assistance programs in the state, (i.e., AFDC, Food Stamps, SSI, HI, DI, and RSI). It is suggested that this ID card, as a minimum, contain the following information:

   a. Name and address of recipient (embossed);

   b. Social Security Number of recipient (embossed);

   c. Case or other state number (embossed);

   Note: This number should correspond with a case number and/or Social Security Number included on the assistance check, Food Stamps, etc.

   d. Color photograph of recipient large enough to cover at least one-half of one side of the card;

   e. Signature of the recipient;

   f. Name and telephone number of the office issuing the card;

   g. The right and left thumb print of the recipient;

   h. Issuance and expiration date of the card;

    i. Any other data necessary to satisfy requirements of the program for which the card is issued; and

    j. A postage free return mailing statement and a warning, in bold type, of the consequences of misuse of the card. The card should conform to standard credit card size so that it can be used in credit card embossing machines.

2. Consider requiring merchants and others who cash public assistance checks to impress the embossed information from the ID card onto the check prior to cashing (i.e., similar to the use of credit cards);

3. Consider sending or transmitting electronically public assistance checks to conveniently located banks where recipients would be required to personally claim and sign for their benefits. This would make it practically impossible for a recipient to obtain a replacement check by falsely claiming that he did not receive the original. This would also substantially reduce the problem of assistance checks being stolen from the mails. This procedure would probably be more practical in metropolitan areas, which the Task Force surveys have shown to be high-risk areas for false ID welfare fraud;

4. Recipients should be required to report stolen welfare checks directly to the local police and to sign an affidavit under penalty of perjury before being issued a replacement check;

5. Identification should be required (ID card as described above) for cashing Food Stamps; merchants should not be paid for fraudulently used Food Stamps;

6. Penalties for knowingly accepting fraudulently cashed Food Stamps should be made severe;

7. Uniform standards for identification of recipients and claimed dependents at intake should be adopted by all states;

8. The security of "breeder" documents such as birth certificates and driver's licenses should be upgraded so as to resist alteration, counterfeiting, and use by imposters. Steps such as mandatory matching of birth and death certificates and carefully controlled issuance should be immediately implemented.

Recommendations to the Federal Government

1. The Federal government should develop comprehensive standards for recipient identification for cost-shared assistance programs, and provide financial assistance to the states in implementing these standards;

2. The Food Stamp Program should be restructured by legislation requiring state sharing of stamp cost and providing more Federal Assistance in costs of prosecuting Food Stamp fraud. These measures would provide the states with incentives for improved control of this program;

3. Food Stamps should be redesigned to resist use of stolen coupons. One means of doing this would be to provide two signature blocks for recipients. One block would be signed upon the receipt of the stamps and the other at the time of use (i.e., similar to the use of Traveler's Checks);

4. Positive identification of recipients should be required prior to approval of applications for Social Security benefits.

REPORT OF THE COMMERCIAL TRANSACTIONS TASK FORCE

ON THE

SCOPE OF THE FALSE IDENTIFICATION PROBLEM AND

PRELIMINARY RECOMMENDATIONS FOR SOLUTIONS

Submitted to

Federal Advisory Committee On False Identification
David J. Muchow, Chairman

May 1976

CONTENTS

SECTION I — INTRODUCTION 81
    Purpose 81
    Scope 81
    Data Gathering 81
    Evaluation of Data 82

SECTION II — THE FALSE ID PROBLEM 85
    General 85
    Losses Sustained 85
    Types of False ID Used 86
    Types of Fraud 87
    Encashment of Checks Stolen from the Mails 88
    Social Obligations — Impact on False ID Fraud 89
    False ID Involvement 91
    Bank Card Fraud 91
    National Association of Security Dealers Survey 93
    National District Attorneys Association Survey 94
    Recommendations 95

SECTION III — PRELIMINARY RECOMMENDATIONS 96
    General 96
    Recommendations from Business and Banking Reps 96
    Technical Devices 97
    Employee Training 97
    Credit and Bank Card Measures 99
    The Dilemma 99
    Current Countermeasures 100
    For the Future 101
    Recommendations from Law Enforcement Reps ... 103

REFERENCES 106

Report Of The Commercial Transactions Task Force

On The

Scope Of The False Identification Problem And

Preliminary Recommendations For Solutions

SECTION I

INTRODUCTION

Purpose

The Commercial Transactions Task Force of the Federal Advisory Committee on False Identification has identified its central concern as the fraudulent use of personal identification in its primary form: over-the-counter sales and bank transactions.

Scope

In order to structure the investigation in a useful and practical way, a model for a commercial transaction has been selected. It is a one-time, face-to-face encounter between a businessman or banker and an individual who wishes to procure goods and/or services using credit or a check, and who remains at the point of sale for only a few minutes. It is recognized that securities and other brokerage transactions generally do not fit into this model because of extensive federal and self-regulatory requirements governing the opening and maintenance of customers' accounts including the strictly applied "know your customer" and suitability rules. Security transactions are not therefore usually executed as a result of a "one time, face to face encounter. However, the model is intended to represent the vast bulk of commercial transactions: those in retail establishments and bank offices. The Task Force has, accordingly focused on the following commercial instruments: checks including Traveler's Checks, Bank Cards, and Securities.

Data Gathering

The main sources of information and statistical summaries used in this report were the business and trade organizations and agencies of government and the law enforcement community most closely concerned with frauds which include false ID. Not the least of the resource available to the Task Force was the personal experience and expertise of the members themselves and that of their associated organizations. Specific sources of information are noted below.

Reports on the scope of the false identity problem were submitted from the following organizations:

American Express
National Association of Securities Dealers, Inc.
Interbank Card Association
Metropolitan Police Department
U.S. Postal Inspection Service
American Bankers Association
National District Attorneys Association

The following organizations conducted formal surveys:

American Bankers Association
National Association of Securities Dealers, Inc.
American Express
National District Attorneys Association

The following have conducted analyses and/or contributed a sampling of records available to them:

Interbank Card Association
Metropolitan Police Department
U.S. Postal Inspection Service

Summaries of the above surveys and analyses are attached to this report. Reference is also made to the following periodicals for a substantial concurrence with the surveys and analyses:

Protection Management & Crime Prevention

    Richard B. Cole
    (W. H. Anderson, Co.)

White Collar Crime

    Chamber of Commerce of the United States

The National Notary, January/February, 1975

    (Commercial)

The Cost of Crimes Against Business

    U.S. Department of Commerce

Identification With & Without Credentials

    American Bankers Association

Evaluation of Data

    The fact that the Task Force is composed of representatives of both law enforcement and business communities led to some disparities in the perception of the false identification problem and in the types of solutions seen as appropriate to the problem. The difference in viewpoint between law enforcement and business interests has been expressed as follows by Task Force Co-Chairman Nathaniel Kossack:

> "In short, the commercial sector is sensitive to the nth degree to cost effectiveness of remedies, which does not permit them to go beyond the recognition of the ratio of losses to the total amount of business. Remedies suggested by business include operational corrections only and do not include referrals to law enforcement which are made routinely. The law enforcement sector has placed the crime of false identification and the crimes using false identification on a low level of priority and have downgraded the traditionally poor "white collar" crime record system to an even lower status. For example, 'paper hanging' is the popular term for check passing and law enforcement tries to avoid the enveloping morass of its volume. Lastly there is an instinctive mutual mistrust between law enforcement and business built up by reason of the conditions of the problem. Commerce complains that law enforcement won't 'protect' them in these cases which can potentially flood the prosecutor's office. Law enforcement does not trust the standards of care (or lack of care) used by commerce and terms the neglect scornfully as 'cost of doing business.' All in all the condition creates a very unsatisfactory record by another artificiality--the anonymous 'third party' victim. That is, the banks do not consider check forgery an important source of loss. The merchant minimizes the loss because he is insured or takes a tax deduction. Like matter, the loss does not disappear; it is merely transferred down the line."

The difficulty of obtaining complete statistical information was also stressed by co-chairman Hollis Bowers in submitting a report to the Task Force on behalf of the business and banking community prepared by himself and Edward Smith, Assistant Director, Communications Group, American Bankers Association:

> "There are as many different statistics on fraudulent commercial transactions involving the use of false identification as there are sources of statistics. Generally speaking, there is a paucity of empirical information as experience following creation of this Task Force has shown that more often than not a commercial enterprise will show losses based on the instruments presented, e.g., checks, without recording the forms of identification used to establish lawful possession of the check instruments. It is believed, however, that the figures cited in this report best represent the presently known situation. In absolute dollar figures the losses due to fraud are tremendous; when averaged out against astronomical bona fide transactions, they seem less imposing. No matter how they may be regarded, the facts and figures reported herein confirm that the commission of the crime using false identification poses a problem for America's bankers and executive, and judicial branches of local,

federal and state governments as best they can within the constraints of social, cultural, and business life in the United States. The recommendations in this report are framed within the real-world limitations of business and banking, and are believed to represent the best possible solutions to the problems of false identification and crime in commercial and banking transactions, given today's business and banking environment."

The description of the false identification problem was constructed from information supplied by members of both business and law enforcement communities. However, the difference in viewpoints is recognized by the presentation in Section III of this report of different sets of preliminary recommendations by the two communities.

SECTION II

THE FALSE ID PROBLEM

General

Commercial transactions take place in a wide variety of locations, ranging from securities houses and stock exchanges to retail and service establishments to the offices of financial institutions. No matter where commercial transaction takes place, however, if the transaction is fraudulent, false identification may be used to add plausibility to an individual's claims and thus to make the transaction possible.

Losses Sustained

Losses resulting from such fraudulent transactions are normally borne by the individual or business that first accepts an invalid instrument, be it a forged check, a check written on insufficient funds or a stolen, altered or counterfeited credit card or security certificate. Thus, the brunt of these losses is suffered by businesses rather than by banks; while a bank may ultimately identify a check as having been forged or a credit card as having been stolen, the loss in the transaction is more often that of the business. Only when a bank is the first acceptor of a fraudulent or invalid check or credit card does the bank itself suffer financial loss.

In dollar terms, this distinction is most apparent. Extrapolating from the results of a 1972 survey, the American Bankers Association (ABA) estimates that in 1974 bank losses due to forgeries totaled approximately $50 million. If that figure is divided by the number of bank offices in the nation (more than 40,000), forgery losses came to only $1,250 per banking office for the year. Significantly, a study of bank operating losses by the Audit Commission of the Bank Administration Institute set 1973 check losses at $45,447,000. Even if these figures were doubled the average per banking office would be quite low. Actual losses certainly vary from bank to bank, depending upon such things as a bank's size, the variety of its services, the quality of its employee training programs, the uniformity of its policy enforcement, the number of transactions in which it is involved, etc. It should be noted also that the number of forgeries reported each year is growing, and to these should be added a broad assortment of other fraudulent "paper" transaction schemes.

In a recent ABA study, stolen and forged checks accounted for the largest proportion--32.4%--of the check fraud schemes. Other check fraud schemes in the order of their occurrence were: counterfeit checks, 23.8%; stolen blank checks, 16.4%; starter checks, 12.5%; split deposit, 9.4%; and others, 5.5%. Retail businessmen estimate bad-check and credit card losses have been approximately $4 billion annually; however, the basis for this figure is not known. Based on

1967 census of business, the U.S. Chamber of Commerce estimates that there are more than 1.6 million business establishments in America. Thus, average annual business loss per establishment are approximately $2,500. Again, individual businesses' losses vary from operation to operation, just as is the case with banks.

Type of False ID Used

In a recent ABA study, the Insurance and Protection Division investigated the fraudulent check schemes reported in state bankers association warning bulletins in 1974. One part of the study dealt with the frequency of various types of false identification. The type of false identification used most often--in 86.35% of the cases-- was impersonation. It was not possible to establish subdivisions of impersonations because of the lack of detail in the reports. This lack was attributed to 2 factors. First, 72.6% of the check fraud checks involved counterfeit checks, stolen blank checks, or stolen and forged checks. In these cases, a form of identification is seldom requested by the bank teller because the check passer persuade the tellers that he is the lawful owner of the check. Second, banks and merchants seldom document the form of ID used when they cash checks for strangers. If there is some doubt about the ownership of a check, the bank or merchant refuses to cash it there are few if any records of the type of ID in aborted cases.

Other types of false ID, in order of frequency, were: driver's licenses, 8.2%; ID cards and other personal identification, both 2.7%; and social security number, 0.05%.

What forms of personal identification are used in these fraudulent transactions? A driver's license and perhaps a "merchant's" or "major" credit card are frequently all that is requested by a merchant. All too often these forms of personal identification prove to be insufficient to protect the merchant. In other transactions, however, many different forms of false identification may be used, depending often on the relative sophistication of the swindlers and their intended victims.

It should be pointed out that many merchants and service operators face a "point of diminishing returns" in establishing the identity of customers presenting checks or credit cards. Obviously, the merchant who refuses to accept either checks or credit cards is automatically alienating a significant portion of the buying public. In the same way, excessive caution or a suspicious attitude in verifying a customer's identity can cause offense and the loss of business. Thus, it can be argued that many merchants accept certain risks and losses due to crimes involving false identification as part of the cost of doing business.

In bank transactions, required signature (or other) verification from the bank's own records for an "on us" check, plus personal recognition of the customer, as well as additional methods of verifying

identity (such as photo ID, thumbprint, computer check on funds in
the account, etc.) help to discourage passers of forged checks, insufficient funds checks (NSF), or split-deposit swindlers. All of these
measures contribute to the positive control of banks' losses as result of crimes involving the use of false identification.

Types of Fraud

    Check Fraud

        Bank Instruments

Americans are now writing more than 25 billion checks a year,[3]
and the total is expected to exceed 40 billion a year by 1980, in
spite of the predicted rapid growth of electronic funds transfer
systems (EFTS).[4]

A 1974 Bank Administration Institute (BAI) study entitled "The
Impact of Exception Items on the Check Collection System" also helps
to add perspective to the scope of the problem of check fraud and related use of false identification.[5] Of the 25 billion checks written
in 1973, the study states,

> "return items accounted for approximately two-thirds of
> one percent of all checks processed--one return for every
> 150 items processed by each bank ... And of those return
> items only 12 percent were identified as missends, forgeries, and unlocated accounts..."

The Federal Reserve System, which clears 85 per cent of all
checks written in the U.S. on American banks, indicates that approximately 100 million out of 1973's 25 billion checks (1 of every
250) were returned for one reason or another. Of that 100 million,
only 25 million finally did not clear--and not all of those were
the result of fraud or crimes involving false identification, since
customer or bank inadvertence causes some bad checks.

The growth in volume of check-writing in the U.S., as well as the
nation's population growth, also helps to put incidence of fraud into
perspective.

A 1970 study by Arthur D. Little, Inc., for the American Bankers
Association points out that,

> "since checks are a form of payment for goods and services and
> are issued against demand deposit accounts, it is reasonable
> to assume that the volume of checks is related to the level of
> production of goods and services and to the number of people
> and organizations holding checking accounts. Employment, income, and various measures of economic flow will also have an
> influence, given any stable pattern of payment habits."[6]

The report shows that by 1968 the number of checking accounts was growing at an annual rate of 4.1 per cent, while the nation's adult population was growing at a rate of only 1.3 per cent. In 1968 also the average number of debits to demand deposit or checking accounts was growing at an annual rate of 12.6 per cent.[7] Thus, with both the number and use of checking accounts growing at a rapid rate, a certain increase in the absolute number of check frauds, including those involving the use of false identification, can be expected.

Encashment of Checks Stolen From the Mails

The Inspection Service of the U.S. Postal Service reports that "false identification use for the cashing of checks stolen from the mails ... most critically affects postal crimes. However, false identification is used in many other postal offenses including, but not limited to, mail fraud schemes such as check kiting operations, credit card frauds and the renting of post office boxes for unlawful purposes."[8]

The U.S. Postal Service figures reported below were gathered in a 20-city sampling carried out by 29 inspectors in 20 major U.S. cities during January and February of 1975. These figures are the result of investigations of checks stolen from the mails; the 20 cities covered were New York, Newark, Boston, El Paso, Seattle, Los Angeles, San Francisco, Buffalo (New York), Philadelphia, Washington (D.C.), Atlanta, Birmingham, New Orleans, Dallas, Chicago, Cleveland, Detroit, Minneapolis, Kansas City (Missouri) and Louisville.

Says the Postal Service Report:

"During Fiscal Year 1974, 140,864 checks with a total face value of $22,331,451 were reported to this Service as stolen from the mails and subsequently cashed. During the two-month (Jan.-Feb. 1975) sampling period, 22,552 checks with a total face value of $4,150,655 were reported as stolen. The sampling covered 5,949 checks."

Information developed from the sampling disclosed that false identification was known to have been used in the cashing of 1,466 of the 5,979 checks. In all probability, false identification was used in cashing many of the other checks but no information was developed to confirm this. <u>Nothing was written on the checks to indicate that any identification was required and the persons accepting the checks were unable to remember what identification, if any, was required.</u> The face value of the checks which were cashed with false identification totaled $315,122,07.[9] (Emphasis added)

In these crimes the three most-frequently used forms of false identification were, in order of use, a commercial photo identification card (496 times), a welfare identification (267 times) and a state driver's license (147 times).[10] Several methods of obtaining false ID were used. False pretense was listed as having been the method used to obtain false identification in the case of commercial photo identification, while stolen welfare ID's accounted for 238 of the 267 incidents reported involving that ID. Further, 101 of 147 of the fraudulently used driver's licenses were stolen.

To take one example of crimes involving checks stolen from the mail--and almost certainly also involving the use of false identification--the Feb. 7 1975, issue of THE AMERICAN BANKER reported that the City of Philadelphia, Pa. alone 10,000 replacement welfare checks with a face value of $1 million were issued monthly in 1972 and 1973. (A grand jury report stated much of the fraud was committed by recipients who falsely claimed not to have received their checks and eventually cashed both the original and replacement checks, though certainly a large proportion of the losses, perhaps as much as half, were caused by outright thefts from the mail.) These reports suggest massive, continuing fraud conducted with false credentials.

These losses were cut by half--or $500,000 per month-- by the simple expedient of requiring all but bedridden or crippled welfare recipients to pick up their checks at their neighborhood bank branches, rather than mailing the checks to the recipients. Nevertheless, welfare check losses of a half million dollars per month in just one major city should constitute an absolutely unacceptable situation.

These figures illustrate the need for constant review of all check encashment operations to design changes which will reduce losses as new needs arise. Such a review should encompass alternatives to "welfare checks" such as direct deposits to welfare recipients' accounts. An explanation of this alternative is contained in Direct Deposit of Federal Recurring Payments, Department of The Treasury, Operations Planning and Research Staff.

Social Obligations - Impact on False ID Fraud

Many banks feel a social obligation to cash checks for certain non-depositors, and this obligation comes to the fore with such financial instruments as welfare and social security checks, as well as salary checks of local, state and federal government employees in the banks' communities. Criteria for proper personal identification in such cases will necessarily vary from community to community, but often an in-state driver's license or employee identification card will be accepted as proof of identification in such cases. In such cases, the bank recognizes that it is running a substantial risk of loss, but feels that it has little real choice in the matter.

Instructions from the U.S. Treasury govern the identity which can be accepted from persons presenting U.S. Savings Bonds to a bank for payment. Among other things, the Treasury requires full notation of the forms of personal identification presented to and accepted by the bank, including such items as military service serial number, date and place of issue and service branch. In the case of drivers' licenses, notation should be made as to what state issued the license what the license number is, and when it was issued.[14] The Treasury Department requires that these measures be taken for it to guarantee payment to banks.

The American Express Company surveyed 6,175 Travelers Cheques regarding identification used with the encashment of the cheques. There were 153 or 2.48% of these that showed some form of identification other than the comparison signature on the check itself. Significantly, over 50% of the identification used were "Driver's Licenses" (see Table I below).

TABLE I

SURVEY OF IDENTIFICATIONS USED IN CASHING TRAVELERS CHEQUES AMERICAN EXPRESS COMPANY

Type – I.D. Used	No. of Items	% No. of Times I.D. Used
Dirver's License	77	50.3
Credit Card	20	13.0
Passport	8	5.2
Vehicle Registration	4	2.6
Social Security	7	4.5
Armed Services		
Coast Guard		
Company Employee I.D.	1	.6
Government I.D.		
Courtesy Card		
Student I.D.		
Bank Book		
Union Book	2	1.3
Unemployment Book		
License (other than Driver's)		
*Other	34	22.2
TOTAL	153	99.7

*Miscellaneous information on back of T/C's, addresses, phone numbers, and other information of which identity of documents presented could not be determined.

In commentary provided, American Express stated that false identification is not a real problem in the encashment of their travelers cheques. Moreover, the acceptance procedures requires in connection with the encashment of travelers cheques merely require the acceptor to witness the countersignature, of the travelers cheque, and compare the countersignature with the original signature. If the signatures are comparable, American Express agrees to honor that travelers cheque. If the acceptor is suspicious of the countersignature, American Express recommends that the acceptor have the person again endorse the travelers cheque on the reverse side and again compare signatures. It is not a requirement that an individual produce any type of identification upon the presentation of a travelers cheque.

American Express has stated that merchants, for their own protection, will require an individual to produce some identificaion at the time of presentation of a travelers cheque, but it is not an American Express procedure. The false identification problem, in connection with the presentation of different types of identification, usually relates to a counterfeit travelers cheque. Over the years, American Express has had a number of individuals who attempted to counterfeit cheques and has noted that on this type of encashment there is more false identification used than in other types of encashment.

False ID Involvement

As noted, the true extent of false ID use in the accomplishment of check fraud schemes of all descriptions must be conjectural for lack of extensive hard data. A notion of the role played by false ID in check fraud activities can be obtained, however, by examination of the data presented in Table II, Check Forgery, Fraud and Embezzlement Data, compiled by the Check Section, Metropolitan Police Department, Washington, D.C. Of note in Table II is the high incidence of detected false ID use in Forgery and Fraud schemes.

Table III from the same source illustrates the type of false ID commonly used, in rank order, and the customary means of acquisition of the false documents.

Bank Card Fraud

The bank card segment of the banking industry continues to grow rapidly although less than in previous years. Growth in retail volume was 26.5 percent in 1974, for example, as compared to 34.6 percent in 1973. In dollar figures, National BankAmericard Inc. and Interbank Card Association (BankAmericard and Master Charge, respectively) report that the 1974 gross volume of billings was $17.6 billion.[11] At the end of 1974, 12,899 banks and 2,182,993 merchant outlets were participating in bank card plans. The average sale was $23.91, and cash advances in 1974 totalled $518 million.

It should be recognized that credit card or bank card fraud is a "second-order crime,"[12] one made possible by an earlier crime;

for example, theft of or tampering with a valid card, or counterfeiting of a card. A 1974 study of The MITRE Corporation, "Security Aspects of Bank Card Systems," identified three categories of bank card fraud, which may also be considered as fairly representing all credit card fraud: misuse of a valid lost or stolen card; use of a counterfeit card; and application for a card by a person with criminal intent.

A typical profile of criminal misuse of credit cards is described by The MITRE Corporation as follows:

"First the cards must be obtained by the criminal, then they can be used to commit fraud. These two crimes can be considered independent events. First a pick-pocket, burglar or thief steals the bank card. (The criminal may not necessarily be concentrating on cards, but if they are available they will generally be stolen.) The criminal will in turn attempt to sell the stolen cards to criminals who specialize in bank card fraud. Since

TABLE II

CHECK FORGERY, FRAUD AND EMBEZZLEMENT DATA

I. FORGERY

A.	Number of compaints.	711
B.	Amount of loss.	$202,109
C.	Number of complaints cleared.	406
D.	Number of arrests	391
E.	Number of complaints where stolen or false identification used.	90%

II. FRAUD (False Pretense - bad checks - confidence schemes)

A.	Number of complaints.	876
B.	Amount of loss.	$333,772
C.	Number of complaints cleared.	499
D.	Number of arrests.	285
E.	Number of complaints where stolen or false identification used.	50%

III. EMBEZZLEMENT

A.	Number of complaints.	143
B.	Amount of loss.	$393,763
C.	Number of complaints cleared.	89
D.	Number of complaints where stolen or false identification used.	15%
E.	Number of arrests	81

stolen cards must be used quickly, a small number of criminals can display a voracious appetite for cards: three to ten cards a week, 150 to 500 cards a year. Moreover, not all of the stolen cards will be used fraudulently; the conditions under which the card was stolen or offered might turn off the criminal buyer."[13]

The statistics gathered by The MITRE Corporation reveal, however, that following a massive wave of bank card fraud in the late 1960's when these credit instruments were introduced, criminal misuse of bank cards has receded since 1970. Total number of bank card fraud cases reported by nine banks in various areas of the nation annually dropped from 5,472 in 1970 to 5,331 in 1974. The real decline, however, is apparent in the drop of the average dollar figure involved in these losses: from $255.64 in 1970 to $164.18 in 1973.

National Association of Securities Dealers Survey

The report submitted by the National Association of Securities Dealers, Inc. (NASD), the self-regulatory agency for the over-the-counter securities market, was based on a survey conducted of its over 3,000 member firms. These members, who are also registered as brokers and dealers with the Securities and Exchange Commission, account for approximately 80 percent of the nation's brokers who transact securities business interstate on registered national securities exchanges and in the over-the-counter market. The NASD received 2,734 replies which represents an unusually high response rate of about 90 percent.

TABLE III

ID USED TO CASH NEGOTIABLE INSTRUMENTS

TYPES OF IDENTIFICATION	HOW OBTAINED
A. Drivers permits	Stolen, counterfeit, false names
B. Credit cards	Stolen, false applications
C. Social Security cards	False names, stolen, counterfeit
D. Government ID cards issued to employees	Stolen, counterfeit
E. Private Business ID cards issed to employees	Stolen, counterfeit, false names
F. Commercial ID cards	Issued by commercial photo companies in any name, no proof of true ID needed.
G. Check cashing courtesy cards	Stolen, false names
H. Bank ID cards	Stolen, false names
I. Selective Service cards	Stolen, counterfeit
J. Governmental Services ID cards issued to recipients	Stolen, counterfeit, false names
K. Passports	Stolen, counterfeit, false names

In constructing its model for commercial transactions, the Commercial Transactions Task Force determined that securities generally do not fit into the definition because extensive federal and self-regulatory rules, designed to prevent the execution of transactions by way of false representation, result in few executions of securities transactions in a "one time, face to face encounter" between a customer and a broker-dealer. (See Section IIA, Definition of the Problem.) The Association recognizes that such situations could occur, however, where a firm was not entirely mindful of its responsibilities under the rules or was careless in the implementation thereof. The study was therefore conducted to determine the extent of the problem. It revealed that during the period 1972-1974 a total of only 18 of the 2,734 responding firms experienced losses as a result of false identification. These firms reported 44 cases in which false identification was cited as the underlying cause of losses. The dollar value of losses reported for these 44 cases totals $563,412.

On the basis of this evidence, the NASD concluded that false identification in the securities industry is only a nominal problem. According to the NASD's report, this low incidence rate of false identification problems is a direct result of the many rules governing the opening and maintenance of customers accounts including the strictly applied "know your customer" and comprehensive suitability rules prescribed and enforced by the various self-regulatory agencies.

The NASD noted, however, that lost and stolen securities, as distinguished from losses resulting from false identification, continue to be a major problem confronting the broker-dealer community and, as such, current efforts in this area must be strengthened and new programs developed. Efforts are underway in this area but such is not the subject of inquiry by this Task Force.

National District Attorneys Association Survey

A national survey of local prosecuting attorneys disclosed that local prosecutors do not have the record facility and capacity to capture false identification data or trend. This points up the fact that adequate records of false identification offenses are no more complete at local levels than at Federal levels.

The prosecutor, in he main, is unmindful and therefore unaware of the false identification problems except in the isolated criminal prosecution. He knows that there is a "flood" of bad check and illicit credit card cases "out there" but his priorities keep him far away. He looks to his police departments for his record information. When he sees the false identification problem, it is mainly in connection with stolen or counterfeited documents and involves credit cards, social security cards, driver's licenses, uniforms and badges, draft cards, police identification cards, passports and visas, alien identification cards, motor vehicle registrations, check books, government or payroll checks, and company identification cards. These are used by individuals (1) to misrepresent their identity;

(2) in conjunction with corroborating false documents; (3) after being altered to correspond with the holder's appearance to assume a new identity either real or imagined and in the commission of a forgery.

It is interesting to note MITRE's* analysis of the use to which false documents are put as derived from NDAA's survey. The fugitive problem alone can develop meaningful statistics. MITRE draws some conclusions from the survey which must be guarded ones in view of the limited responses to the survey as a source for false ID conclusions.

"...the number of incidents of the use of false identification per year equals approximately 1% of the population.

"...reported impact of false identification incidents when averaged by dollar value per incident would appear to be about $400 per incident. Based on these figures, the cost of false identification incidents (known to prosecutors) annually to the USA would approach $90,000,000. The most significant item of analysis is that only 20% of the prosecutors reported maintained any records under their own cognizance.

Recommendations

    a. Require more substantial identification.

    b. Educate clerical help in the methods used by holders of false identification.

    c. A better system of identification, e.g., social security card to include a color photograph and fingerprint of the holder.

    d. Tighter controls over the issuance of governmentally authenticated documents. (i.e., birth certificate, driver's license, social security cards)

It is obvious the prosecutor sees the problem as one involving theft and counterfeiting and the use of the false identification to commit a serious offense. Unfortunately in the latter, his case records do not disclose those incidents involving false ID as an instrument of prosecutable crime. The average prosecutor views the multi standards and loose approach of merchants to ID issues with some scorn, and will not give a high priority to these cases even when the proof is more than marginal. The prosecutor often tends to view the false ID problem primarily as an operational one better suited for industry and commerce control. To that end he prosecutes a minimum of such cases presented. He views the law as adequate.

---

*An informal paper presented to the Task Force.

SECTION III

PRELIMINARY RECOMMENDATIONS

General

The preliminary recommendations of the Commercial Transactions Task Force are presented in two separate sections, reflecting the differences in viewpoint between the representatives of the commercial and the law enforcement communities. The two disparate viewpoints are considered generally complementary and the recommendations of these two groups are not, in general, mutually exclusive although the operational premises do differ greatly.

The first section, representing the ideas of banking and business members, emphasizes the precautions against false ID fraud that are practical at the present time, without recourse to additional technology or legislation. The second section, developed from the suggestions of District Attorneys and other law enforcement personnel, stresses improvements in technology and customer education.

Section III also includes a brief discussion of Automated Personal Identification, a developing field of technology by which individuals may be identified by comparing values of measured personnel characteristics against values of other characteristics previously stored in a computer data base. This type of identity verification requires no identification documents.

Recommendations from Business and Banking Representatives

General

Many swindlers operate almost completely without credentials of any sort, depending instead on their persuasive abilities, their power to "con" their intended victims. They may, for example, try to confuse or embarrass a bank teller or retail sales clerk with a series of special requests -- changing and re-changing money, loud claims to be bona fide depositors, split deposits (which should in themselves be a warning signal), etc. -- and hope that in the resulting confusion, the teller or sales person will fail to follow procedures for establishing identity and validating credentials in order to cash a check or accept a credit card. Thorough employee training and well-conceived management policies are probably the best preventive measures against such swindles, and such training programs should include strict adherence to the bank's or business's identification policies and procedures and support by management when employees adhere to the prescribed procedures.

Identification With and Without Credentials, a publication of the American Bankers Association, notes that "no bank has a legal obligation to cash a check drawn on another bank. Although every bank is required to pay on demand a bona fide check drawn on itself, every bank is also pemitted to delay cashing any check for any of at least five reasons."[15] These reasons also constitute an excellent checklist for verifying a presentor's identity and his right to cash the check he presents. Acceptors should verify that:

"1. the signature is genuine;

2. the maker has sufficient funds on deposit to cover the check (in the case of an 'on us' check);

3. payment has not been stopped;

4. the presenter is adequately identified; and,

5. the bearer of the check has title to the instrument."[16]

Technical Devices

Many highly sophisticated technical devices now exist which can aid in the later identification of persons who have fraudulently presented a check or credit card to a banker or merchant. These include fingerprint identification devices and photo records of the presenter and of the instrument. While these devices may help to identify and track down criminals, they do not necessarily deter actual fraud.

The possiblilities for machine control of credit card fraud are almost endless - and, in some cases, very expensive. They range from laser analysis of materials embedded in the card to machine-reading of metallic wafers sandwiched inside the card to optical scanning. The central concerns are to prevent tampering with a card's magnetic strip, which is the crucial operative portion of a card, and to ensure that only the lawful owner of such a card can use it. It appears that developing technology will be able to meet the challenges posed by the criminal world. A full exposition of recent developments in this area is included in Security Aspects of Bank Card System, a study by The MITRE Corporation for the American Bankers Association.[21]

Employee Training

The old dictum, "know your customers", still serves as the best preventive to crimes committed with false identification.

Many common sense procedures that do not require special equipment also are available to merchants and bankers. White Collar Crime, published by the Chamber of Commerce of the United States, stresses this point.

 Acceptors of credit cards -- especially their money-handlers, such as cashiers -- can play a particularly critical role in preventing credit card fraud and in enhancing an establishment's reputation for being 'no pushover': Check the dates on the card indicating when it becomes valid and when it expires. Refer to issuer's card cancellation bulletin. Note if the card appears altered or defaced. Compare the signature on the card with that on the sales slip. Call the issuer's special authorization number if any of the danger signals...(such as multiple purchases on the same day, split purchase to keep under authorization limit, etc.) arouse suspicions...Keep card imprinters and blank charge slips under tight control. Drop floor limits, in retail operations, to zero in selected departments occasionally. Keep cashier areas well-lighted to discourage unauthorized transactions and to reduce errors. Select as a cashier someone who has basic intelligence and who has been well trained. Do not allow waiters to imprint charge slips. Investigate customer allegations of mishandled credit card transactions.[17]

Employees' lack of familiarity with basic identification documents such as drivers' licenses can make the use of false identification easy for criminals. Employees may even not know how to read codes on a driver's license or what to look for to verify the authenticity of a document presented to them. White Collar Crime recommends the following steps to limit check fraud losses:

> Safeguard blank checks and check-writing equipment. Require identification before cashing checks. Do not accept the following for identification purposes -- Social Security cards, business cards, club cards, letters. Become familiar with the driver's license issued by your state and neighboring states (one source for this information is Drivers License Guide, published annually by Drivers License Guide Co., 1492 Oddstad Drive, Redwood City, Calif. 94063). Certain built-in features -- such as year of birth as part of the license number -- may help you identify counterfeits presented for identification. Compare not only the person's signature but also his appearance with what is indicated by his identification document. Do not accept an updated or postdated check, nor one that is dated more than 20 days previously. Require personal checks to be made out for the exact amount of the purchase...Witness endorsements. If the check is already endorsed, have it re-endorsed...Do not cash checks written in pencil.[18]

Other steps listed in White Collar Crime are designed to prevent fraud committed with an individual or merchant's own checks. "Inspect the middle and back sections of check books, especially after a theft has been committed on the premises...Safeguard bank statements and cancelled checks. They reveal your bank balance, signature, and check design...Do not prepare checks with typewriters utilizing 'lift off' ink."[19]

98

Credit and Bank Card Measures

Security measures instituted by the issuers of credit cards and bank cards have contributed substantially to the reduction of losses due to frauds involving their cards. While some of these measures depend on the intelligent cooperation of merchants and their sales staff, others operate strictly internally, for example, through computer-monitoring to detect card usage that varies from certain norms.

White Collar Crime outlines some of these measures:

> Shortly after cards are mailed, a follow-up inquiry is sent to determine if the card arrived. This simple procedure has cut fraud losses substantially, thanks to the timely information it elicits. To reduce even further the possibilities of theft from the mail, some issuers use registered mail when cards are sent to 'high risk' Zip code zones.
>
> Various security features are built into cards on a periodic basis as an anticounterfeiting measure.
>
> Computers of many card issuers can alert officials if a cardholder's spending departs from his traditional pattern; if so, the cardholder may receive a phone call from the issuer and be asked to confirm if his card is still in his possession.
>
> Depending on an acceptor's fraud-loss record, he may be required to seek authorization -- via phone -- from the issuer before honoring a user's card in transactions above a prescribed amount. Computers of some issuers are able to relate the fraud-loss experience of an establishment to that of others in the same area. Where losses seem out of line, investigators may be sent to the scene. Card cancellation bulletins, which contain the numbers of stolen or lost cards, are sent to acceptors periodically and rewards are given to those who pick up unexpired cards listed in these bulletins. Experimentation is now under way with regard to computer-linked terminals that employ scanners to validate cards at the point of sale.[20]

In addition, credit card issuers now scrutinize applications for their cards very closely, and investigations may take as long as six to eight weeks. Such careful and thorough investigations help to avoid the issuance of cards to persons who may have falsely identified themselves and have made their application with criminal intent.

The Dilemma

Clearly, there is almost no limit to the amount of identity verification that can be carried out in commercial transactions. In general, the rules outlined above work equally well for merchants and bankers. Certainly, some identity documents simply should not be accepted; among these are commercial personal photo identification cards, library cards, blood donor cards, and Social Security cards. Tellers and sales persons should be familiar with the documents that they do accept so that a customer's identity can be properly established. On the other hand, the more restrictive a merchant's check-cashing or card-accepting policy, the more limited his field of customers becomes. Likewise, the more time-consuming it becomes to cash a check in a bank or to open a checking account, the less happy a banker's customers are. The dilemma is the same for bankers and businessmen. If you make your operation totally fraud-proof -- and it probably can be done -- you run the distinct risk of making it customer-proof, too.

This fact helps to explain why it is easy to open a checking account today. In general, no more than a Social Security number is required; lacking that, a student ID or other such card will be accepted. The bank customer supplies two specimens of his signature, and the account is opened. Why is it so easy? Simply because a bank wants to provide a broad spectrum of customer services, and it is through a checking account that an individual receives his first introduction to full banking services. The same factor affects merchants, who must do business to stay in business. Each operator must balance for himself the relative risk and profit potential in each decision on accepting a check or credit card. Refusing to accept checks, credit cards or certain personal identification documents may cut a merchant off from a certain portion of his market; on the other hand, the wholesale, indiscriminate acceptance of checks, credit cards and personal ID's very likely will expose a merchant to considerable losses.

In the same way that merchants are reluctant to risk offending a legitimate customer, bankers are reluctant to make it more difficult to open checking accounts. The provision of bank services -- personal, installment and business loans, trust services, bank cards, etc. -- constitutes an important source of bank revenues. In addition, the funds available to banks from customers' deposits in checking accounts have become very important for loan purposes. Finally, it should be pointed out that the overwhelming majority of bank transactions are legitimate; this has been true historically and continues to be true.

Current Countermeasures

Recognizing the dangers of fraud inherent in the free operation of checking accounts, some banks have taken steps to control these possibilities. For example, most banks mail printed checks to their customers, rather than handing them over on the spot, since this helps to verify the customer's address. Many banks have eliminated courtesy checks. Banks also may require a telephone number and verify the customer's residence by a phone call. Some banks have eliminated counter checks, and the Federal Reserve System no longer handles counter checks through its clearing houses. The intent of these steps is to minimize the possibilities of check fraud, as well as to achieve standardization for processing purposes.

While banks' losses due to check and credit card fraud continue to diminish each year, even as the nation's annual volume of checks doubles each decade, it must be recognized that merchants' losses have in some cases reached intolerable levels. However, when the preventive steps outlined in earlier sections of this report are followed carefully and conscientiously, they can significantly reduce merchants' losses from check and credit card frauds.

Of all the methods currently available to protect the security of "cash machines" now in use by some banks, the "Personel Identification Number" seems to be the most effective. This is a number known only to the customer and the computer. When the customer inserts his magnetic card into the cash machine, he must punch out his Personal Identification Number in order to verify his identity before any transactions can take place. When electronic funds transfer systems (EFTS) achieve wider acceptance, it is possible that the use of a Personal Identification Number at point-of-sale, on-line computer terminals could effect the same goal of ensuring security of the system. The use of the Personal Identification Number is by far the cheapest and most effective system now available, The MITRE Corporation concluded.[12]

(More information on EFTS is available in A Digest of Electronic Funds Transfer Systems Thinking Today, a publication of the American Bankers Association.)

For the Future

It is concluded that procedures currently known and available, if consistently used by merchants and bankers, could signficantly and satisfactorily reduce losses due to crimes involving false identification. These procedures, which involve authentication of identification documents at the time of the commercial or banking transaction, have been outlined above. As previously noted, banks which have followed such procedures have successfully minimized losses due to fraud.

The eventual implementation of electronic funds transfer systems will also help to reduce such crimes. When, for example, the funds involved in a supermarket transaction can be instantly debited to the customer's account and credited to the merchant's account (at the same moment that the computer codes verify the customer's identity), the problems of bad checks and customer inadvertence, as well as many of the problems of forgery, will be virtually eliminated. These new systems, however, will required their own elaborate safeguards; such protective devices and procedures are now under development and hold great promise of success.

In addition, direct deposits through electronic funds transfer systems are helping to diminish the possibilities for fraud, since if a check is not physically existent it cannot be stolen and cashed fraudulently. For example, the Treasury Department is currently experimenting with direct deposits to Social Security recipients in certain Southeastern states; it is hoped that such direct deposits of recurring government payments will eventually be established nationwide. Again, direct electronic payments through privately-operated automated clearing houses are eliminating check fraud and achieving significant economies in processing of payments. Minimization of losses remains a major goal of these innovations, and as each new electronic funds transfer system enters use, steps are taken to avoid computer crime as well.

Many banks now excercise tight control over information and materials likely to make check and credit fraud possible, within their commitment to provide full customer service. This control includes refusing to cash checks for non-depositors and refusing split deposits unless approved by management personnel. It is felt that, on the whole, retail merchants have also moved in recent years to curtail losses caused by crimes involving false identification.

Clearly, it would be desirable for all banks and retail establishments to keep detailed records of documents accepted for purposes of authenticating an individual's identification. This procedure can be useful in locating persons who presented invalid instruments. The usefulness of this procedure depends, however, on the ability of sales persons and tellers to correctly evaluate identity documents presented to them and to make thorough notations regarding those documents. A business or bank which suffers chronic major losses due to fraud perpetrated with false identification could well consider tightening policies and upgrading employee training in the evaluation of identification documents, as well as noting the identification presented.

<ins>Legislative Solutions</ins>

Given both bankers' and merchants' need to maintain the free flow of business activity, it is felt that restrictive legislation which might adversely affect the present freedom of business activity is not needed. Bankers and merchants through establishment of firm policies and procedures can minimize their losses due to fraudulent transactions. On the other hand, any legislation which could speed the apprehension, prosecution and punishment of criminals using false identification would be welcome. Certain recent legislation, notably PL 93-495, which was sign into law in October of 1974, moved in that direction. That law doubles the maximum sentence for credit card crime from 5 to 10 years and lowers the threshold at which federal prosecution may be triggered, as well as expanding the list of federal credit card crimes.

Agency and Institutional Process

It is felt that thought should be given to the question of who issues and guarantees the validity of personal identification documents. For example, as noted by other Task Forces of this Committee, what steps are taken to verify the identity of an applicant for a driver's license or for a duplicate license? Again, crosschecks of birth and death certificates are desperately needed, since it is apparent at present that would-be criminals can use states' and localities' laxity in this area to establish convincing false credentials with relative impunity. How difficult is it to forge or misuse these documents? Experience leads to the conclusion: "not hard enough."

Active Prosecution

How often is anyone prosecuted for counterfeiting or fraudulently possessing Federal, state or local identification documents? Too often the illegality of these acts is forgotten, and prosecution takes place solely on the basis of some other crime committed by the individual.

Institutional Policy and Intelligence Activities

Constant review by banks and retail establishments of their check cashing and credit card accepting policies remains a must, since the ingenuity of criminal elements never flags. Monitoring of criminal trends by banks and businesses must be carried out constantly so that commercial practices regarding financial instruments can be adjusted to meet the ever-new challenges of the criminal world. However, as noted above, most of these actions are best carried out by individual banks and businesses, taking into account local needs, business potential and risk exposure.

Recommendations from Law Enforcement Representatives

General

In their attempts to combat crime based on false identity, police and prosecutors are often frustrated by insufficient resources and conflicting priorities, compounded by the feeling that the problem is aggravated by the "loose" practices of their banking and commercial constituents. From the surveys of District Attorneys and the statistics of the Washington, D.C. police, the following conclusions may be drawn:

1. The most prevalent methods of obtaining false identification appear to be theft and counterfeiting.

2. The losses to the individual businesses and enterprises are "small" in comparison to the total industry business but awesome when grouped together as a national figure.

Also important are the "losses" net calculable in monetary terms, such as those resulting from the ability of dangerous criminals to operate unmolested thanks to false identification documents.

3. The cost effectiveness argument is the swindler's best friend.

4. Law Enforcement has no clear picture of the problem and will not until its record keeping capacity is improved.

The recommendations which appear to gain the most support are:

1. Improving the integrity of the most frequently used documents -- birth certificate, driver's license.

2. Instituting a national identification document as proposed by the Passport Office.

3. Developing standards to be used by check cashers, sellers, etc. The sanctions can be in the collectability of insurance and, in the less frequent situation, the declination of prosecution. This recommendation depends on:

    (a) The improvement of selected identification documents.

    (b) The willingness of industry and commerce to adopt the standards even though the "cost effectiveness" presents some problems. (No one expects industry to lose money, but a large initial investment followed by success can turn the cost "effectiveness" argument around.

4. Developing an educational program that can reach in simple understandable terms the clerk, the cashier, the merchant in their crowded life. The other side of the coin is an educational program to induce the honest citizen to use only selected types of identification. This will help militate against the argument that strict standards chase the customers away.

5. Developing of a uniform record-keeping system for law enforcement to use to measure the scope of the problem and suggest changes in priorities in the implementations of existing laws by law enforcement.

Automated Personal Identification

Automated Personal Identification,[22] a study by the Stanford Research Institute's Long Range Planning Service, provides some

possible long-range solutions to the problem of false I.D. This
document has a message even for the non-skilled. It makes a strong
case for <u>fully automated devices</u> for identification (as distinguished
from manual) verification of credit by clerks resorting to an I.D.
document or to an electronic computer terminal. In the fully automated system one or more personal characteristics (e.g., fingerprint,
weight, voice, memory) will be used as identification. The study
contains a recognition of all the psychological constraints. It
is even contemplated that a "no card" automated system could be devised where a person to be identified would supply a name or identification number and access is made to a personal data record in the
central file.

REFERENCES

1. *Federal Register*, Vol. 39, No. 205, October 22, 1974, pp. 37515-37516.

2. Roy Jacobus, official statement to Task Force on Commercial Transactions.

3. Robert H. Long, Charles R. McClung and Walter W. Stafeil, *The Impact of Exception Items on the Check Collection System* (Park Ridge, Ill., 1974), a report by the Bank Administration Institute, p.3.

4. *Major events in evolution of EFTS are occurring with rising frequency*, report in *Banking*, a journal of the American Bankers Association (May 1975).

5. Same as footnote 3, pp. 3-6.

6. Arthur D. Little, Inc., *The Outlook for the Nation's Check Payments System, 1970-80*, a report to the American Bankers Association, (Boston, Mass., 1970), p. 114.

7. Ibid., p. 115.

8. William J. Cotter, chief inspector, U.S. Postal Service (letter to Hollis W. Bowers of American Bankers Association, 1975).

9. "False Identification Usage in the Cashing of Checks Stolen from the Mails", a report by the U.S. Postal service (Washington, D.C., 1975), March 1975, pp. 1-2.

10. Ibid., p.2.

11. ABA Bank Card Letter, a newsletter of the American Bankers Association (Washington, D.C., 1975), April 1975.

12. M. Ferdman, D. W. Lambert and D. W. Snow, *Security Aspects of Bank Card Systems*, a report to the American Bankers Association by The MITRE Corporation, (Bedford, Mass., Dec., 1974), I. p. 15 (study to be released).

13. Ibid., p. 15.

14. *Protective Bulletin* (Washington, D.C., 1950), American Bankers Association, Sept. 1950.

15. *Identification With and Without Credentials*, a publication of the American Bankers Association (Washington, D.C. (1974), p. 7.

16. Ibid., p. 7.

17. *White Collar Crime*, a publication of the Chamber of Commerce of the United States (Washington, D.C. 1974), pp. 75-76.

18. *Ibid.*, p. 77.

19. *Ibid.*, p. 77.

20. *Ibid.*, p. 76.

21. M. Ferdman, D. W. Lambert and D. W. Snow, *Security Aspects of Bank Card Systems*, a report to the American Bankers Association by The MITRE Corporation, (Bedford, Mass., Dec., 1974), I, p. 15 (study to be released).

22. Raphael, David E. and Young, James R., *Automated Personal Identification*, Stanford Research Institute, Report No. 539, Dec. 1974.

REPORT OF THE FUGITIVES TASK FORCE

ON THE

SCOPE OF THE FALSE IDENTIFICATION PROBLEM AND

PRELIMINARY RECOMMENDATIONS FOR SOLUTIONS

Submitted to

Federal Advisory Committee On False Identification
David J. Muchow, Chairman

May 1976

CONTENTS

SECTION I — INTRODUCTION 111
    Purpose 111
    Scope 111
    Data Sources 112

SECTION II — THE FUGITIVE FLASE ID PROBLEM .. 113
    Classes of Fugitives 113
    The Militant Terrorist/Revolutionary 113
    The Juvenile 113
    The Traditional Criminal 114
    Types of False ID 114

SECTION III — FUGITIVE CRIMES 115
    General 115
    Fraudulent Check Passing 115
    Passport Frauds 116
    Social Security Account Card Frauds 116
    Narcotics Trafficking 116
    Illegal Aliens 117
    Insurance Frauds 118
    Credit Card Schemes 118
    Traveler's Check Schemes 119
    Automobile Theft Rings 120
    Bank Fraud and Embezzlement 121
    Internal Security 122

SECTION IV — PRELIMINARY RECOMMENDATIONS   124

ATTACHMENT I — INTERPOL RESPONSE 125

Report of the Fugitives Task Force

on the

Scope of the False Identification Problem

Recommendations for Solutions

SECTION I

INTRODUCTION

Purpose

　　The task of the Fugitives Task Force was to examine the ways in which and the extent to which false identification is used to impede the apprehension of fugitives in our society.

Scope

　　In examining the nature of fugitives, it is necessary to examine and categorize the crimes or potential crimes which have engendered the assumption of fugitive status. It is axiomatic that maintenance of a fugitive status is much aided by a false identity and that continued criminal activity while in this state may -- most often does -- require a series of false IDs. Otherwise, the original false ID becomes as harmful to the fugitive as a true ID would be.

　　It is assumed that the fugitive state begins at the planning stages of a crime. When the intent assumes reality, acquisition of a false ID with which to commit the crime impedes correct and early assignment of responsibility for the crime, and aids the criminal in maintaining a fugitive status.

　　Accordingly, the use of false identification by fugitives to avoid detection and arrest or linkage to a previous criminal record, to remain in a covert status, or to aid in the commitment of further crimes, were the areas of primary concern to the Task Force.

　　The extent of this issue is vividly set forth in a statement by the Montgomery County Sheriff's Department of Dayton, Ohio. It states:

> "There is not a standard from which you can draw specific types, as criminals' use of false ID has become commonplace among persons engaged in all walks of illegal activity. A common belief that alias names are restricted to forgery types of crime is a gross misconception. The growing and thriving business in underworld sale of false identification

and related items has become so standard that not only does
the common thief have ready access to any type of false ID
he wishes, but also he finds the going street price within
the easy reach of his budget. As a result, it is possible
for anyone to assume an identity other than his own and to
provide upon demand almost any type of identification to
substantiate it.

"All areas of criminal activity, including persons perpetrating forgeries of checks and credit cards, persons who
know they are wanted for criminal violations, persons who
are engaged in organized criminal activities, arrested persons, traffic violators, and even high school students who
want to change their ages for beverage purchases, are known
to purchase and use ID of this type.

"For practical purposes, it is safe to assume that any and
all documents that can be used for the identification of a
true name can and are being used to provide false identification. State operators' permits, credit cards, social
security cards, employment cards and badges, draft cards,
hospitalization cards, fraternity and special club cards
are among the most common; however, it is not unusual to
find stolen or counterfeit birth certificates, baptismal
records or passports in the possession of known criminals.
We have encountered multiple pieces of ID, all in the same
alias name, in the possession of suspected persons, and in
several cases, multiple ID in different names thus allowing
the person to assume a variety of identities.

"The Montgomery County Jail has an average of eight to ten
persons booked into the jail each month under alias names.
These figures are based on known statistics."

Data Sources

The methods utilized to gather information included surveys of
selected sheriff's offices, metropolitan police departments, Interpol, and the Federal Bureau of Investigation. Sources of other
information included the Administration of the Internal Security
Act of the Committee of the Judiciary, United States Senate, and
the 1973 and 1974 FBI Annual Reports.

Quantitative data on the number of incidents of each type of use
of false identification by fugitives were not obtained, since this
type of information is rarely recorded or assembled for easy retrieval. Fugitives guilty of major crimes are seldom additionally
charged with fraudulent use of false identification, since this is
usually only a misdemeanor. In other cases, prosecution for fraudulent use of false identification is not often undertaken, since
the fugitive is not a criminal (e.g., minor runaway, illegal alien).

SECTION II

THE FUGITIVE FALSE ID PROBLEM

Classes of Fugitives

Three classes of fugitives are usually associated with the use of false identification. These are:

1. The militant terrorist or revolutionary;

2. The juvenile; and

3. The traditional criminal.

They are discussed below.

The Militant Terrorist/Revolutionary

The militant terrorist or revolutionary has espoused a cause varying from racial protest to overthrow of the government through armed force. Protest actions eventually take the form of criminal activity requiring the militant to "go underground." After going "underground", the militant assumes a false identity to avoid detection and arrest and to remain in a covert status. The false identity is supported by false documents sufficient to create the illusion of authenticity. Activities are continued under the assumed identity until arrest or until the false identity becomes linked to the true identity, whereupon another false identity is assumed. If arrested, the militant may utilize the false identity documents to avoid being connected to previously committed illegal acts.

The Juvenile

The juvenile assumes false identity for a number of reasons. These range from the borrowing of a friend's driver's license to purchase alcoholic beverages or to gain access to a restricted movie, to the acquisition of a means by which to escape from an unhappy home or institutional environment. Juvenile fugitives impose an expense upon society through the additional burden their escapes place upon police and juvenile authorities. However, this type of fugitive is considered outside the scope of the Task Force's deliberations. Unfortunately, a juvenile fugitive seeking to establish a permanent false identity may become involved in narcotics or vice through association with those who possess the capability to provide false identity documents. Such involvement would bring the juvenile fugitive back under the Task Force's consideration as a criminal.

The Traditional Criminal

The third class of fugitive is the criminal who engages in crime for personal gain. Included in this class are: bad check passers, fraudulent users of credit cards, robbers, rapists, shakedown artists, confidence men, drug traffickers, embezzlers, murderers, illegal aliens, etc. Some of the activities of these criminals and their use of false ID is discussed in great detail in the reports of the Commercial Transactions Task Force (Appendix A2) and the Government Payments Task Force (Appendix A1). Accordingly, only a brief description is given here.

Criminals may assume a false identity before or after the commission of a crime, usually dependent upon the nature of the criminal activity. Some criminal activities are independent of identity (e.g., murder, burglary, theft); some depend upon a known identity, usually factual (e.g., embezzlement); and some are dependent upon assumed identity (e.g., forgery, fraudulent use of credit cards, passport violations, illegal entry into the country). Criminals may carry false identification to avoid being linked to previous criminal activities. Escapees from penal institutions almost always assume a false identity. A growing area of concern is the use of false police identification by criminals to gain access to premises for the purpose of committing crimes such as robbery and rape or to shake down pimps, prostitutes, addicts or homosexuals.

In New York City, false impersonation of police officers is a growing phenomenon. During 1974, incidents involving police impersonators increased by 88 percent. Arrests for this crime increased from 215 in 1973 to 265 in 1974, an increase of 23 percent.

Types of False ID

Types of false identification utilized by all three classes of fugitives are similar. These include: birth certificates, driver's licenses, Social Security cards, Selective Service cards, and credit cards. It is important to recognize that the first four of these are used purely for identification by the fugitive and are documents which are issued by government entities. Birth certificates and driver's licenses are state and local documents; Social Security and Selective Service cards are federal documents.

Other documents which have been used in the establishment of false identity are: marriage licenses, school records, voter's registration cards, medical assistance records, and military identity cards. Since all of these are also documents which are issued by governmental entities, the problem is addressable by government itself.

SECTION III

FUGITIVE CRIMES

General

There are a number of crime types which are commonly used to maintain a fugitive or which are the reason for fugitive status in the first place. Some of these crimes are explored in greater detail by the FACFI Task Forces on Commercial Transactions, or Government Payments
They are discussed in the context of this report because many are repeating crimes which become a source of livelihood to the criminal and are, in fact, necessary to maintain a fugitive status; if forced to work in the ordinary way, many fugitives would have difficulty avoiding detection and arrest. Accordingly, a circular pattern develops in which a crime is committed, sometimes with the aid of false ID, causing the individual to become a fugitive for which continued use of false IDs and accomplishment of false ID related crime is essential.

It is worthwhile, therefore, to consider the nature of crimes in which false ID has some effect. The most prominent types are discussed in the following subsections.

Fraudulent Check Passing

The passing of fraudulent checks has long been an investigative nemesis of all areas of law enforcement. Checks have without question become one of the most important transactional instruments in the world today. A recent publication issued by the Public Information Department, Federal Reserve Bank of New York, reported: "We use checks to pay $9.00 out of every $10.00 we spend. Today, there are about 91 million checking accounts in the United States."

The best estimates of check losses through false ID (forgery and counterfeiting) which FACFI has been able to obtain place annual losses at over $1 billion per year. These estimates have been derived from a Bank Administration Institute study[1] and the results of a special study[2] on check fraud. Further details on check fraud are contained in Section 4 of the FACFI Final Report.

---

[1] Bank Administration Institute, The Impact of Exception Items on the Check Collection System (Park Ridge, Illinois), 1974.

[2] Editorial Staff, "How Big is the Bad Check Problem?" Security World, July/August 1974.

115

Passport Frauds

Recent congressional testimony[1] asserts:

> "There is no mystery as to why persons engaged in criminal activities desire U.S. passports and will go to any lengths to obtain them. In most cases, these individuals are already known in their true identities by law enforcement agencies, and some of them are being sought as criminals by law enforcement agencies. To continue their illegal activities, they need new identities."

Also:

> "In the fiscal year 1973, we discovered 449 domestic frauds... in addition to the frauds perpetrated by drug traffickers and illegal aliens; we also have frauds perpetrated by militant groups, confidence men, and fugitives."

The example, as set forth above, is one of many which would be cited by this Task Force relative to fugitives' use of fraudulent passports as part of false identification documentation.

Social Security Account Card Frauds

Social Security Account Cards issued today carry the following notation: "For Social Security and Tax Purposes - Not for Identification." Numerous Social Security Account Cards are, however, being obtained daily by fugitives as part of their false identification documentation. Fugitives recently arrested by the FBI and other law enforcement agencies have frequently been in possession of these cards. Investigations have revealed the criminal element utilizes the Social Security Account Card as an integral part of false identification documentation and in many of the instances such cards were secured in the names of deceased infants.

Narcotics Trafficking

Investigations conducted by all of law enforcement undeniably reveal the narcotics trafficker and false identification are nearly inseparable. Narcotics trafficking is certainly big business. To confirm this, the following statistics covering hashish seizures are set forth.

---

[1] Partial testimony of Mr. William E. Duggan, Chief Legal Division, Passport Office, Department of State, before the Senate Subcommittee to Investigate the Administration of the Internal Security Act and other internal security laws of the Committee on the Judiciary, October 3, 1973.

During the aforementioned hearings[1] conducted by the Senate Subcommittee of the Committee on the Judiciary, Mr. John R. Bartels, Jr., then Acting Administrator, Drug Enforcement Agency (DEA), testified that in 1968, 534 pounds of hashish were seized and in 1972, 30,094 pounds.

During these hearings, Mr. Bartels also testified, relative to a case involving the Brotherhood of Eternal Love (BEL), a drug trafficking organization that,

> "Their mode of operation placed heavy reliance on the use of false passports; and with their financial resources and false documents, they achieved complete international mobility. During the period of their successes, we have estimated on the basis of hard intelligence that approximately 24 tons of hashish was smuggled into this country."

Illegal Aliens

Investigations conducted by the Immigration and Naturalization Service (INS) reveal there is an ever-rising trend of immigration frauds. This trend is well-illustrated by the following INS statistics:

> "For the Fiscal Year 1965, 5,233 fraud investigations were completed, and for the Fiscal Year ending June 30, 1974, there were 16,676 Service investigations of indicated immigration frauds."

INS has also recently reported:

> "During the intervening years of rising immigration fraud activity, fraudulent schemes have been encountered incident to nearly every method and category of entry into the Unites States and have extended to the misrepresentation, altering, and counterfeiting of the majority of entry and status documents issued to aliens seeking entry and/or residence in this country. The arrangers and vendors of such schemes and related documentation normally work independently or in small groups, both in the United States and abroad. Behind these frontmen, however, there is frequently an organized group of document counterfeiters, alterers, and thieves who specialize in stealing valid documents for alteration and copying. It is these groups who keep the vendors supplied with their merchandise."

---

[1] Ibid.

To further show the magnitude of this problem the following information was set forth in the November 16, 1974 issue of the "Washington-Star News":

> "In the 12-month period that ended June 30, the Immigration and Naturalization Service caught 788,185 illegal aliens. Eighty-eight percent, or 693,084 of them, crossed the border without papers. They were 'wetbacks,' although the term is a misnomer because most simply walked across and never came near the Rio Grande."

The remaining 12 percent - 95,061 people - were tourists or students who overstayed their visas and just tried to blend into the community.

Insurance Frauds

The criminal element, utilizing false identification, has also found this area of endeavor quite lucrative. Investigations have revealed that individuals obtain automobile insurance under a number of false identities with several insurance companies. Once the necessary insurance is obtained, these individuals then falsely claim loss due to thefts of clothing, cameras, jewelry, and other expensive merchandise.

As an example, evidence of criminals' involvement in insurance fraud and the use of false ID, the following case is cited.

During the summer of 1974, information was received that an unknown individual in California had requested and obtained the birth certificate of a deceased infant. Subsequent investigation developed that the unknown subject had (1) subsequently secured a United States passport under this deceased infant identity; (2) had a paramour who had also adopted the identity of a deceased infant, and (3) had secured a fraudulent passport using this false identity.

Extensive investigation ultimately identified both individuals, who were subsequently arrested on charges of obtaining fraudulent passports. Once the male subject was identified, it was determined he, under his true name, was in the process of suing an insurance company for over $5,000,000.00 for an alleged injury; the subject settled for $75,000.00.

Credit Card Schemes

Credit cards present a fertile field in which the criminal subject, utilizing false identification, can operate. Of the high volume of arrests being made throughout the United States each day, in many instances the arrested subject has in his possession a copy of "The Paper Trip[1]," a well-publicized underground "How to do it" book.

---
[1] The Paper Trip, anonymous author, undated.

"Paper Trip" explains in detail how to secure and utilize false identification. On page 21, the following is set forth under the caption "Credit Cards":

> "Professional ID inevitably includes the full range of commercial cards -- both paper and plastic. Although a few companies are beginning to use customers' photos on the card, as a class they generally have no personal ID information whatever. Your name, signature, account number, and dates between which the card is valid are about as far as they go in providing individual data. The rest is stored in their computer file, based on your original credit application.
>
> "In today's increasingly cashless society, credit cards are becoming the controllable link between people, income, and property. They are immediately accepted for a multitude of specific financial jobs, and in most transactions they are the only ID required. THE PAPER TRIP considers them ID and thus includes here its own ideas on how to obtain them. What you do with them is of course your own business.
>
> "The first rule, unquestionably, is DON'T USE SOMEBODY ELSE'S CARD!! Much too dangerous and criminal. Infinitely better is to get the credit card companies themselves to send you their cards, but under any name you choose. The credit companies and banks who issue these cards are very anxious for your trade, and double anxious to issue the real card to all those who qualify. So the secret is, OBTAIN YOUR OWN CARDS, LEGITIMATELY!!! You do this by studying their brochures and applications to determine more or less what they expect. Even though your new name will have no existing record, a $400.00 minimum deposit at a large bank will put you on the road to a geometrically expanding credit rating."

Traveler's Check Schemes

Traveler's checks offer the criminally inclined excellent opportunities to finance their criminal activities, as well as afford them financial resources while in a fugitive status.

As evidence of the above, the following example is cited to show the criminal's use of this type of scheme.

During the latter part of 1971, an individual was arrested by a local law enforcement agency on the West Coast for perpetrating a larcenous traveler's check refund operation. At the time of his arrest, the subject furnished a name which was believed to be fictitious. Subsequent investigation revealed the arrested subject had assumed the identity of a living individual, who was not in any way involved in any criminal activities.

For an approximately three-month period, the arrested subject refused to furnish his true identity. He subsequently agreed to cooperate with police authorities and at that time furnished his true identity.

The arrested subject, when interviewed in detail, confessed his extensive involvement, during 1970-1971, in a fraudulent traveler's check scheme in which he used a number of false identities, some fictitious and some of deceased individuals. The subject advised that during the year he used eighty to one hundred different false identities. He added that during his most prolific activity, he used approximately thirty different identities in almost daily refund frauds. From the monies obtained, the subject was able to finance his criminal status with considerable ease.

Automobile Theft Rings

Investigations have revealed that automobile thefts are constantly being perpetrated by criminals operating under the protection of false identification. The following is a case in point.

During the early part of 1974, an individual was arrested on the West Coast on a charge of obtaining a fraudulent passport. Investigation revealed this individual had assumed the identity of a deceased infant and had completely documented this identity, which included the securing of a fraudulent passport. Following the arrest of this individual, further investigation revealed he had apparently been directly involved, since 1968, in a car theft ring involving expensive automobiles. There is every indication that as many as 55 to 60 vehicles, valued from $15,000.00 to $20,000.00 each, were involved in this operation.

The FBI reports[1] relative to interstate automobile theft rings:

> "Interstate automobile theft rings operated by skilled professionals continued to receive a large measure of FBI attention under the Interstate Transportation of Stolen Motor Vehicle (ITSMV) Statute in Fiscal 1973.
>
> "A multimillion-dollar auto theft ring investigation was successfully concluded on May 25, 1973, when a Federal Jury in Bowling Green, Kentucky - after hearing testimony for eight weeks from 982 witnesses - returned guilty verdicts on 19 persons on the charge of conspiring to violate ITSMV Statute. Two other subjects previously had entered guilty pleas.
>
> "The trial culminated more than two years of investigative work by the FBI in cooperation with state and local law inforcement agencies.

---

[1] 1973 Uniform Crime Reports.

"During Fiscal 1973, FBI investigations of ITSMV violations resulted in 2,017 convictions. Sentences imposed amounted to 3,934 years' imprisonment, 2,093 years in probationary sentences, and 716 years in suspended sentences. Fines totaling $95,900 were assessed. Some 1,154 ITSMV fugitives were located."

Bank Fraud and Embezzlement

Criminal fugitives have not neglected this area of endeavor in their criminal activities. Each day, investigations show that individuals are traveling from state to state establishing bank accounts under assumed identities. Once such accounts are opened, they use such accounts to support a variety of criminal endeavors, such as check "kiting," split deposit fraud, and loan frauds.

The 1973 FBI Uniform Crime Reports included the following information relative to this matter:

Some 1,064 convictions resulted from FBI investigations as amounts of money involved in bank frauds and embezzlements continued to increase.

These FBI investigations[1] vary from inquiries into mysterious disappearances of nominal amounts of money to complaints involving defalcations of major sums.

During the past decade, the number of convictions in these cases has almost doubled - 577 in Fiscal 1963, as compared to 1,064 in Fiscal 1973. The amounts of shortages have increased yearly, from $14.1 million in 1963 to $135.6 million in Fiscal 1973. The number of cases reported also has climbed over the decade -- from 2,469 to 6,787.

White collar crimes -- offenses committed by persons in a responsible position in government and private enterprise -- increased dramatically during the past fiscal year.

In a report to the Commercial Transactions Task Force, the Washington, D.C. Police Force assert that about 15 percent of the embezzlement cases which come to their attention involve the use of false ID. It can be reasonably inferred, therefore, that the use of false ID is a nontrivial component of this crime.

There is increasing evidence of a new form of false ID bank and business embezzlement found involving computer controlled accounting

---

[1] It should be noted that a majority of fraud and embezzlement cases are not subject to FBI investigation.

of credit transactions. In this context, a computer expert and bank executive[1] recently stated:

> "The base form of an asset is no longer necessarily a 40 ounce gold bar; now assets are simply magnetic wiggles on a link."

The fraudulent use of computer keys, codes, passwords and the like, and abuse of computer files, data, and operating systems is a false ID crime and one with enormous loss potential.[2] Further, these frauds and embezzlements are difficult to either detect and counter or protect against, and there is some evidence[3] that victimized institutions are often reluctant to bring charges against their own employees for fear of losing public confidence.

There is also evidence that this method of fraud is either growing rapidly or being detected with greater frequency, and that criminal organizations are becoming involved as well as technically clever and innovative individuals.[4]

In summary, we repeat the conclusion of a recent newspaper article[5]:

> "The potential rewards and the seeming ease of escaping any heavy punishment have made credit fraud an enormous secret industry."

Internal Security

Investigations clearly reveal the use of false identification plays a prominent role in internal security areas. This is evident in information set forth in the 1973 FBI Annual Report, under the subcaption "Weatherman," which reads, in part, as follows:

> "Weatherman began in 1969 as a faction of the militant Students for a Democratic Society (SDS). Thereafter, Weatherman quickly evolved into a separate Marxist group which is dedicated to the violent overthrow of the government. In early 1970, Weatherman members

---

[1] Richard Mills, Vice President, First National City Bank, "Waiting for the Great Computer Rip-Off," Fortune, July 1974.

[2] Op. cit., Fortune, July 1974.

[3] Ibid, one reported case involved a loss of $5 million. A cited 1971 study found that twelve cases of computerized bank embezzlement averaged $1.09 million apiece - about ten times the average embezzlement loss.

[4] Ibid.

[5] "New Credit Risks: Loan Swindle, Subverting Data Banks Spread," The Wall Street Journal, April 18, 1976.

abandoned their offices and residences and entered underground status. They did so to better pursue armed struggle against the Government.

"Since entering underground status, Weatherman has used sophisticated techniques of false identities and clandestine communications.

"During a speech made on November 11, 1974, when making reference to Weatherman, FBI Director Clarence M. Kelley commented, 'Since early 1970, the Weather People have been underground. By underground, we mean their adherents live under aliases, using false identification papers and fabricated life histories.'"

With every passing day, investigations vividly reveal criminals are entering fugitive status on an ever-rising basis. This aspect is certainly borne out by the following data as reported in the 1974 FBI Annual Report:

"An all-time high of 37,891 FBI fugitives were located during Fiscal 1974. Those apprehended included bank robbers, kidnappers and deserters, as well as felons, wanted by local authorities. Some 3,478 were sought at the specific request of state and local authorities for violations of the Fugitive Felon Act.

FBI Director Kelley states:[1]

"To the law-abiding citizen, the specter of expanding lawlessness cannot help but provoke anguish - and for good reason. It is his tax dollars that have financed the war on crime, and it is his safety, possessions, and community that are mainly threatened by lawlessness...

"To combat crime effectively requires at the outset a realistic examination. One reality of crime is that repeat offenders are at the core of the problem. Studies of criminal histories reveal convincing evidence that as much as two-thirds of all offenses are committed by recidivists -- persons who have been arrested for and convicted of crimes previously."

---

[1] "Law Enforcement Bulletin," Vol. 43, No. 11, November 1974.

SECTION IV

PRELIMINARY RECOMMENDATIONS

Since most of the type of documents used in the establishment of false identifications are issued by governmental agencies, the following steps could contribute to a solution of this problem:

1. Applicants for any of the type of identification documents listed above should be required to provide adequate proof of identity prior to receiving the requested documents;

2. More rigid safeguards should be imposed upon the storage of blank forms so they might be less prone to theft;

3. The quality of identification documents could be improved so that falsification through alteration or counterfeiting would be more difficult. This could be accomplished through the incorporation of a photograph, a fingerprint, and a coded number which could incorporate identity features of the issuee;

4. The public could be better educated in methods for verifying the identity of the identification holder and the reasons why they should be concerned about this problem;

5. Procedures for checking criminal identity upon apprehension could be improved so that the true identity of the suspect could be ascertained prior to the release from custody;

6. Stiffer laws could be passed with regard to users of false identity. Such laws could include:

    a. Removal of applicability of the statute of limitations when the use of false identification is involved in a crime;

    b. Refusal of probationary sentences to users of false identification in the commission of a crime;

    c. Stiffer sentencing of users of false identification; and

7. Laws could be passed which would impose severe penalties upon anyone who is convicted of manufacturing, selling, distributing, or passing false identification documents.

ATTACHMENT I

INTERPOL RESPONSE

International

The General Secretariat, International Criminal Police Organization - Interpol, through the United States National Central Bureau - Interpol, furnished information concerning the problem of false identification on an international basis, which includes counterfeiting and/or altering of passports, drivers' licenses, and other identification cards and the methods which appear to provide a maximum degree of protection against counterfeiting and/or altering of these documents.

For the alterations, a legitimately issued document is obtained from the rightful owner by theft or other means, or a legitimate document is obtained from the issuing agency by fraudulent means, usually followed by alteration of the text and signature of authentic passports or other forms of identification, such as drivers' licenses, identity documents, letters of credit, and so forth. The forgers principally use three methods: scraping, erasing and washing, or by the addition or substitution of lines, letters, photographs or entire pages.

For the counterfeits or complete production of a false document, the counterfeiters use basically the same methods/procedures as currency counterfeiters, such as acquisition of a genuine document followed by obtaining plates or type molds by photograph or moldings, manufacture of stereotype plates by engraving or printing, using typographic or planographic methods.

Methods which are considered to provide a maximum degree of protection against counterfeiting or altering documents are as follows.

1. At the Manufacturing Stage

   An identification document should be printed on special paper, "protected," made of pure pieces and producing no fluorescence under ultraviolet light. This paper should be of strictly maintained thickness and quality and should have well-patterned watermarks.

   Security indications, such as fluorescent "planes," can be incorporated into the paper during its manufacture. The printing should be carefully done, preferably using typographic methods. A security background, printed with thin or reactive ink, in the form of cartridges, in the areas to be filled out by identification data or signatures, will greatly complicate modifications through washing and scraping.

The numbering should be typographically done with a numerator with specially engraved characters, having original designs that are easily recognizable; for numbering purposes, the use of fluorescent ink will permit rapid verifications, using very simple materials.

The cover should be strong, semi-rigid and, if possible, include a seal in relief.

The cover and pages should be bound in such a way that it is difficult to remove or add pages (the use of special rivets seems advisable).

2. At the Stage of Issuing the Document

The use of indelible ink of a special sort is desirable, but in practice difficulties might be encountered.

The lines containing the identification data should be completed by conventional signs, so as to avoid the addition of letters.

The use of a dry stamp is indispensible, but it should have subtlety (fine and closely drawn lines along the border, for example) which makes it difficult to pick up the print of the dry stamp.

The photograph should be attached with glue that is insensitive to heat, water, and most solvents; synthetic polymerized glues seem to provide the most guarantees.

Finally, a process which seems likely to prevent the substitution of photographs consists in placing the print of one of the holder's fingers partly on the passport and partly on a border of the photograph.

A review of the problem of false identification on an international basis since 1947 reveals that it has been a continuing problem.

At an Interpol Symposium held in December 1974, the problem of false drivers' licenses was considered. The delegation from Spain reported that through international cooperation they had recently detected a large number of counterfeit drivers' licenses of Portugal, France, Germany, Morocco, Venezuela, and Argentina. The ensuing discussion revealed that of some 20 countries represented, almost every country has a large number of false drivers' licenses in existence. They ranged from complete counterfeits to genuine licenses altered and genuine licenses obtained through the use of false identity documents. The use of these false driver's licenses, frequently accompanied by the use of fraudu-

REPORT OF THE FEDERAL IDENTIFICATION DOCUMENTS TASK FORCE

ON THE

SCOPE OF THE FALSE IDENTIFICATION PROBLEM AND

PRELIMINARY RECOMMENDATIONS FOR SOLUTIONS

Submitted to

Federal Advisory Committee On False Identification
David J. Muchow, Chairman

May 1976

CONTENTS

SECTION I — INTRODUCTION 130
   Purpose 130
   Scope 130
   Data Gathering 130
   Evaluation of Data 131

SECTION II — THE FALSE ID PROBLEM 134
   Application Phase 134
   Eligibility and Enablements 134
      Visa 134
      Immigrant Visa 134
      Non-Immigrant Visa 134
      Alien Registration Receipt Card (Form I-151) 135
      Nonresident Alien Mexican Border Crossing 135
      Passport 135
   Application Fraud Estimates 136
   Analysis of Detected Application Fraud Data 138
   ID Documentation and Verification 138
      Visas 138
      INS Documents 139
      U.S. Passport 140
   Customs Verification of Entry Documents 140
   "Use" Phase 140
   Fraudulent or Incorrect Usage 141
      Visas 141
      Entry Without Visas 143
      Passport Frauds 143
      Summary 143
      INS Documents 144
   False ID "User" Profiles 151

SECTION III — SOCIETAL IMPACT AND COSTS 154
   General 154
   Welfare Costs 154
   Health Service Costs 154
   Income Tax Losses 155

Balance of Payment Losses 155
Illegal Alien Jobs 155
Criminal Activity 155
    Smuggling 155
Fugitives 158
    False ID Investigations and Prosecutions 158

SECTION IV — COUNTERMEASURES TO CRIMINAL USE OF FALSE ID 160

General 160
Detection of User Fraud 161
    False Alien Documentation 161
False Entry Without a U.S. Passport 162
Application Phase 163
    Visa Office 163
    INS 163
    Passport Office 164
Use Phase 164
    Visa Office 164
    INS 165
    Customs Service 166

SECTION V — RECOMMENDATIONS FOR AMELIORATION OF THE FALSE ID PROBLEM 167

General 167
International Agreements 167
Domestic Practices 167
    Prosecution of Cases 167
    Inter-Agency Cooperation 168
    Inter-State Activities 168
    Training and Education 168
    Legislation 169

Report of the Federal Identification Documents Task Force

on the

Scope of the False Identification Problem &

Recommendations for Solutions

SECTION I

INTRODUCTION

Purpose

The Federal Documents Task Force was formed to examine the use of personal documents issued by the Federal government in false identification assisted crimes. Both an identification of the scope, crime patterns and societal cost of the problem and suggested solutions are main elements of the work of this group.

Scope

There are many documents of interest to the Task Force. These include particularly The Passport, the Alien Registration Receipt Card[1], the Nonresident Alien Mexican Border Crossing Card[2], and the Immigrant and non-immigrant Visas affixed to passport documents. For purposes of this study, the visa is considered a document.

The principal Federal organizations associated with either the original issuance of these documents or their subsequent evaluation are: The U.S. Passport Office (PPO), the Immigration and Naturalization Office (INS), the Customs Bureau and the Department of State.

Other Federal agencies, bureaus and offices concerned with the false ID problem in one fashion or another include the Department of Transportation, the U.S. Coast Guard, the Selective Service System, the Drug Enforcement Agency (DEA) and the Federal Aviation Administration, all of which are represented on the Task Force.

Data Gathering

Data acquisition was mainly by structured survey. Useful additional information of direct importance to the work of the Task Force was extracted by some organizations (notably the Visa Office and the INS) from extant reports and statistical summaries.

---

[1] Immigration and Naturalization Service (INS) Form I-151.
[2] INS Form I-186.

In general, the fraud problem has been divided into three components as follows:

1. Application Frauds, dealing with various misrepresentations in acquisition of documents in the ordinary way;

2. Document Frauds, having to do with alteration or counterfeiting of the documents themselves; and

3. User Frauds, concerning impersonation and imposture in the conduct of transactions involving the use of IDs.

There were several primary sources of data. These included:

1. In-house studies made by the INS;

2. Surveys and extant data by the Visa Office;

3. Case sampling by the DEA; and

4. Case studies by the Customs Service.

The Visa Office contacted all visa issuing posts and solicited the views of Foreign Service and Consular Officers associated with the visa issuing process. Based upon this information, maximum and minimum projections were made bounding the visa fraud problem.

The INS followed the same pattern but provided, rather than a range, firm estimates of the extent of the problem based on data collected by the service.

The report from the DEA was based on a random sampling of 589 cases from which 17 were identified as involving false ID.

Data supplied by the Customs Service is based entirely on specific cases; all involved alien traffickers.

Passport Office data was similarly compiled from specific cases.

Evaluation of Data

Hard data on the false ID issue is not often readily at hand. All contributing sources note the difficulty of retrieving false ID data with precision and surety. In many cases, recourse was made to informed opinion of officials long associated with the problem.

Proper interpretation of hard data which does exist is further hampered by problems of detection. The Passport Office, for example, has data on detected passport frauds; the extent of successful frauds can be only guessed at.

Estimation of societal cost, either directly accruing from false ID crimes or indirectly in benefits, services, the value of activities of alternate to false ID investigation and the like, are as spotty as the false ID estimates themselves. The Visa Office reports:

> "...there is great need for statistical data on the scope and dollar impact of the fraudulent identity problem in general. The small fraud unit operating within the Visa Office has not at this stage had the opportunity or the manpower to collect statistics on the problem from a wide range of sources. The officer issuing visas overseas is often overworked and has neither time nor resources to undertake the kinds of investigations and surveys which would produce the needed information. VO is in the process of seeking additional data concerning fraud from the INS and has requested additional manpower in the area of fraud."

In many cases, the ID fraud is not reported as having been considered "peripheral" to the major crime committed. The Customs Office reports:

> "The exact data on the incidence of use of false identification is not obtainable because our statistical procedures do not provide for its retrieval. False identification is the modus operandi used by the perpetrator to commit the Customs violation, i.e., smuggling narcotics, etc. Customs violations are carried in over thirty investigative case categories and reported under same."

Further, there are anomalies in the data reported and the estimates arrived at by expert opinion. For example, the DEA sample, admittedly limited, suggested a figure of about 3% as representing the degree of false ID association with the international cocaine trafficking cases studied. The expert opinion of a DEA official, on the other hand, was that 80-85% of all drug trafficking cases were attended by false ID use. Customs data suggest 79%. All respondents agree that false ID does represent a problem and that the documents their organizations issue, certify, inspect, or otherwise administer are subject to this abuse. Further, there are strong indications in the data that do exist, that false ID abuse of the studied documents is increasing year by year, a phenomena more fully explored in subsequent parts of this report. The societal effect in either dollars or any other measure is less documented and documentable since many of the effects are secondary or tertiary.

There is general agreement among the expressed suggestions for solution to or amelioration of the problem, however, despite different organizational viewpoints and perceptions of the problem. These matters are also discussed in subsequent sections of this report.

The false ID problem is intimately associated with criminal activity on both the purely domestic and international spheres. Some portion of the costs of these illicit activities must be accordingly attached to false ID, which is without any serious question, an enabling influence of substantial aid to the conduct of this activity.

SECTION II

THE FALSE ID PROBLEM

The documents of concern to this Task Force fall generally into two classes: those which enable international movement by individuals either into the U.S. or out of it across international boundaries; or those which entitle individuals to certain social benefits. In the former class are the U.S. Passport, various visas, alien registration documents and the like. In the latter category is the Social Security Registration Card.

There are other Federal documents, U.S. military ID for example, which may be subject to occasional false ID abuse but the preponderance of evidence suggests that most of the false ID problem is associated with the passport, alien documents, and the Social Security card. In order to adequately set forth the false ID problem relative to the documents of interest, it is necessary to expand on a number of issues relating to their proper and improper acquisition and use. Accordingly, the following material addresses these issues. Included are: descriptions of the ordinary document application process including the ID documentation required by the issuing agency or office; the nature and extent of the verification process employed; the degree of fraud detected; and the intended use of the documents. Also included are discussions of document abuse, including particularly the criminal activities in which these documents play a role.

Application Phase

The following material is presented document by document.

Eligibility and Enablements

Visa

Immigrant Visa - The immigrant visa permits the recipient to settle in the U.S. as a permanent resident, to engage in gainful employment as and where he chooses, and eventually to become an American citizen. In general, the immigrant visa applicant must establish that he is entitled to an immigrant visa either as the close relative of an American citizen or permanent resident alien; or that he is a worker or professional whose skills are in demand in the U.S. as certified by the Department of Labor; or that he falls into one or another category that would entitle him to an immigrant visa (i.e., longstanding U.S. government employee, refugee).

Non-immigrant Visa - The non-immigrant visa permits an alien to apply for entry into the U.S. for a temporary stay for a particular purpose: tourism, business, study, transit, international organization employment, crewmember, for example. The vast majority of holders of these visas are not permitted to work and are required to have a residence in a country outside the U.S. which they have no intention of abandoning. The application requirements for most kinds of non-immigrant visas include an application form, a photograph, a valid passport, and proof of entitlement to the non-immigrant status for which application is made.

Alien Registration Receipt Card (Form I-151)

While INS issues many different documents, this discussion will be limited to Form I-151, Alien Registration Receipt Card, and Form I-186, Nonresident Alien Mexican Border Crossing Card.

The Form I-151 is a part of the Immigrant Visa and eligibility therefore is determined by the American consular officer abroad. The entry data is added to the form at the time of the alien's entry to the United States. This card is evidence of the alien's registration and admission as a lawful permanent resident. Aliens having such cards are entitled to take employment in the United States.

Nonresident Alien Mexican Border Crossing Card (Form I-186)

A Form I-186 may be issued to any eligible citizen of Mexico for entry to the United States as a temporary visitor for periods not to exceed 72 hours and is limited to travel within 25 miles from the Mexican border. Holders of this card are not entitled to take employment in the United States. The citizen of Mexico must apply in person for such card to an Immigration Officer at a border port or to an American Consular Officer in the interior of Mexico. He is interrogated as to his eligibility for such card and must support his application with evidence of Mexican citizenship and residence. As a minimum, he must present a regular Mexican passport, a provisional passport issued by the governor of a state in Mexico or a Mexican Form 13, a document issued by the Mexican Immigration Service.

Other ID evidence considered would be previously issued INS documents, birth and baptismal certificates.

Passport

A person who desires to obtain a U.S. passport must apply for it using a stipulated form which must be executed before a person authorized by the Secretary of State to accept passport applications in the U.S. or abroad. Under certain stipulated conditions, a person who has been issued a U.S. Passport within 8 years may complete an application and send it to the Passport Office by mail. The conditions of such "mail-in" applications are strict -- to prevent possible fraud. At the present time such mail-in applications do not present a fraud problem and constitute about 12% of the total volume.

Since U.S. passports may be issued only to nationals of the U.S., applicants must prove by documentary evidence that they are nationals. Also they are specifically required to establish their identity. The nationality requirements are statutory (22 USC 212).

The identity requirement is specifically mentioned in the Regulations (22 CFR 51.28).

The application and evidence are adjudicated by experienced Passport Examiners. If nationality and identity are satisfactorily established, a passport is issued. If not, the applicant is required to submit additional evidence or an investigation is undertaken.

Application Fraud Estimates

Estimates of the scope of the fraudulent application problem are given in Tables, I, II, and III below for visas, INS documents and U.S. Passports, respectively. For visas and INS documents, the degree of the fraud problem is estimated as a fraction of the total number of applications processed. For Passport another figure is given: Applications per detected fraud.

TABLE I

Visas

Document Type	Applications Per Year	Rejected[1] Applications	False[2] Applications (est.)
Immigrant Visa	325,000	20,000	6%
Nonimmigrant Visa	3,000,000	220,000	7%

[1] In most cases, although outright fraud may not have been attempted, the applicant has sought to deceive the consular official in some way.

[2] Estimated at 5-10% of the rejected applications. The larger figure is used in Table I.

TABLE II

INS Documents

Document	Applications Per Year	Counterfeits Detected	Altered Cards Detected	Imposter Use of Unaltered Cards Detected	Percentage of False Application
Alien Registration Receipt Card (Form I-151)	364,000	4,074	1,361	2,086	2%
Nonresident Alien Border Crossing Card (Form I-186)	170,331	585	1,623	6,160	5%

TABLE III

U.S. Passport

Year	Applications	Applications from High Fraud Potential Groups[1]	Detected Application Fraud	Applications Per Detected Fraud
FY71	2,311,789	462,356	288	1605
72	2,605,321	521,064	300	1736
73	2,769,549	553,903	499	1233
74	2,471,461	494,292	553	893

---

[1] It was determined that a high fraud potential group can be defined consisting of first time, native-born applicants between age 18 and age 40. There is no known fraud in official government travel applicants and none of any magnitude in family group applications. Combining all these factors, the high fraud potential group is estimated at 20% of total applicants.

Analysis of Detected Application Fraud Data

Since application fraud is only a part of the false ID problem and the data given are based on detection of fraud at application, the true figures are probably higher than those shown. For entry visas and the two most important INS documents, these figures range from 2% to over 7% of total applications.

Passport application fraud has, over the period cited, increased 92% while the number of total applications increased by only 6.9%. The Passport Office, however, notes that a fraud detection training program was begun in the spring of 1972 and has resulted in the increased detections in FY's 73 and 74.

It is not possible to assess with surety either the extent of application fraud for the subject documents or the time trend from the data presented here. It should be noted, however, that the numbers are not small and the estimates conservative.

The degree of concern which should be attached to these figures must rest with a linking of fraudulent immigration, entry into the U.S. or passport acquisition with specific criminal activities and their societal impact. This issue is treated in subsequent sections of this report.

ID Documentation & Verification

There are a number of documents which may be used to establish ID and status for purposes of acquiring visas, INS documents and passports. In the case of U.S. entry documents which may originate from virtually any area of the world and be processed by consular officials remote from the U.S., document verification may be especially difficult because of the sheer variety of document types encountered. The following discussions set forth these issues in some detail.

Visas

The fact that the whole process of application for a visa and verification of identity factors occurs outside the U.S. presents special problems. In many cultures of an individual name itself is a source of difficulty: surnames may be unknown, or rarely used; a person may be given only one name if he comes from a relatively undeveloped area; there may be comparatively few names in use, so that duplication of name is common; names may be changed for luck, religious reasons, whim, marriage, when honors are granted or trials successfully undergone; names written in scripts other than the Roman may be Romanized in different ways at different times, and so on. Conditions and cultures in many countries make reliable documents hard to obtain or difficult to verify or assess: foreign officials who issue documents may be bribed or persuaded to issue false documents; private persons (relatives, employers) may have no interest other than that of the requester in mind and may issue a false letter or document attesting to an ability, an employment record, a financial condition, a relationship, that may have no bearing on reality. Many life events in non-western societies occur without benefit of civil documentation; in other societies the requirement of documentation is honored largely in the breach. Language is often a problem in that translations of documents are time-consuming; in addition, letters or certificates in English may have been signed by honest officials or private individuals who were deceived by the applicant and had no real idea what the document contained; data keeping on the part of foreign national and local governments may refuse to assist the consular officer in attempting to verify government documents; applicants may be unable or unwilling persecution, and the issuing authority may have no interest in providing documents to such persons.

Examination of the alien identity and status documentation always or frequently required to obtain either the Immigrant or the Non-Immigrant Visa reveals:

1. The variety is enormous ranging from birth certificates, passports and national identity documents to property deeds, bank books, divorce and marriage certificates and vehicle registrations. There are nineteen types noted by the Visa Office.

2. Of the nineteen ID document types always or sometimes requested, thirteen are reported to be subject to frequent fraudulent use, five sometimes and only one (the Selective Service Card) with no fraudulent use reported.

Pressures of workload and shortages of investigative personnel at many posts often preclude verification of the authenticity of documents except in cases where there are clear indications of fraud. Routine verifications are generally not possible, though random checks of apparently authentic documentation are sometimes carried out. However, in high fraud areas, some routine verifications of documents are made and investigations launched when indicated.

INS Documents

Identity evidence is required prior to the issuance of any of the INS documents. It consists of previously issued INS documents; immigrant and non-immigrant visas; official foreign documents including birth certificates, police records, military records, marriage licenses; divorce decrees; death certificates; fingerprint checks; affidavits; depositions; and identifying witnesses in some cases.

Authentication of documents is dependent on the specific type of document presented with an application. INS personnel are trained and experienced in questioning and interrogation techniques. This method of examination is generally sufficient to establish the validity of a document and legitimacy of the bearer. Additional authentication measures, including a field investigation, are taken if reasonable doubt exists after questioning an individual.

U.S. Passport

The United States passport is, by definition, a document of identity and nationality. Consequently, a person applying for such document must establish, by documentary evidence, these two factors. Identity is normally established by a reliable document issued by a governmental agency which contains a photograph or physical description and signature. U.S. citizenship is established generally by the submission of a certified copy of a birth certificate showing birth in the United States. The applicant must fill in a passport application.

The evidence of identity and birth is examined by the passport agent accepting the passport application along with the information furnished in the passport application. If the passport agent is satisfied with his short interview of the applicant and his examination of the documentation of identity and citizenship, no verification procedure is undertaken. If, however, the passport agent notices what are called "symptoms of fraud," verification procedures will take place. This verification will depend upon the questionable factors which the agent notices. The verification procedures can be in the nature of telephone or written communication throughout the United States to the source of the documents submitted. It could also include the same type of communication to verify addresses or references given in the application.

In some cases, the verification is undertaken by the investigatory agency for the Passport Office.

Customs Verification of Entry Documents

The Customs examination is the last step encountered by the arriving passenger before entry is made into the United States, whether he is a citizen or an alien. A U.S. citizen is processed by the Passport Office and furnished a passport for travel abroad. An alien is processed abroad by the State Department for issuance of a non-immigrant visa to enter the U.S., and his foreign passport is examined by Immigration at the time of entry. Therefore, the Customs Service does not question the validity of a Declaration as identification, unless a Customs violations is detected, (i.e., narcotic smuggling). Passports are the document most frequently involved in the use of false identification.

"Use" Phase

General. Both non-immigrant and immigrant visas are used to apply for entry into the U.S. They are presented at ports of entry to inspection of the INS. The Alien Registration and Mexican Border Crossing documents are used to effect entry into the U.S. or to remain here and take employment.

A U.S. Passport is used to enter and/or depart the U.S. (8 USC 1185) or primarily for use in traveling or residing abroad. The Supreme Court has stated that the U.S. Passport is a political document which, in effect, identifies the bearer as a national of the United States and requests foreign governments to give to the bearer all lawful aid and protection. In cases of civil strife abroad, the U.S. Passport can be the difference between life and death. It is also the document in which foreign governments place their visas showing that the bearer is entitled to enter such foreign country.

Aside from its official use as described above, it has common usage as identity evidence in commercial transactions in the U.S. and abroad.

Fraudulent or Incorrect Usage

Visas

Both kinds of visas have one primary purpose and use: to permit the bearer to apply to enter the United States. Immigrant visas and a few categories of non-immigrant visas permit the bearer to be gainfully employed in the U.S. But some persons who enter the U.S. on visas which do not permit them to work nonetheless seek and often find employment. If an alien is discovered working illegally, the penalties levied on him and on his employer are not severe, and the chances that he will be detected are small. These aliens who seek and find unauthorized employment take jobs that American citizens and those legally authorized to accept employment could fill. In addition, many illegal aliens pay no taxes on their illegal earnings and consume substantial welfare benefits. The societal impact of illegal immigration is discussed in Section III of this report.

It is difficult to attach a precise figure to the visa aspects of the illegal alien problem. Not all illegal aliens presently in the United States entered on visas; in fact, if INS apprehension statistics are representative of the illegal alien population as a whole, probably no more than 10-15% of the illegals presently in the U.S. had any contact whatsoever with the visa issuance process. In addition, not all aliens who become illegals intended to violate their status when they applied for visas and their applications had no fraudulent aspects. Not all applicants who did intend to violate status had to resort to identity fraud to do so.

1. Counterfeit non-immigrant visas - A survey of reported counterfeit visas for the period March 1970 through August 1972 revealed 287 confirmed cases. It is generally assumed that where there is one counter-

feit, there is more than one, and that for every counterfeit detected, others escape detection. The estimated number of counterfeits for the countries and time involved in the survey (estimates made by the posts involved in the reported cases) range from 1,800 to 7,000. If it is assumed, based on this survey, that the average number of attempts (some successful) to use counterfeit visas ranges from 90-350 per month, the average is 1,080 to 4,200 per year.

2. Refusals - At least 250,000 visa applicants are finally refused visas each year. It is conservatively estimated that 5-10% of these refusals involve some element of identity fraud[1]. This adds 12,500 to 25,000 to the total.

Table IV, below, gives the Visa Office's estimated breakdown of the false identification problem:

TABLE IV

False ID Use by Aliens in Visa Fraud

		Annual False ID Use by Aliens	
		Low Estimate	High Estimate
1.	Counterfeit visas	1,080	4,200
2.	Aliens Apprehended	4,000	4,000
3.	Aliens not Apprehended	8,000	20,000
4.	Changes of Status	2,250	2,250
5.	Refusals	12,500	25,000
6.	Aliens Excluded	26,500	26,000
	Total	54,330	81,950

The scope of the false identification problem as it pertains to visas is thus 50,000 to 80,000 instances per year of the use of false identification. The former figure is a conservative estimate and the latter a moderate estimate of the scope of the problem.

---
[1] Some visa-issuing posts put this figure at 50% or higher.

Entry Without Visas

It has been estimated that there are from four to twelve million illegal aliens currently in the United States. Six to eight million is now the official INS estimate. Although the preponderance of these aliens are believed to have effected illegal intry between the ports of entry along the Mexican border, many have effected their entry into the United States with false identification. A larger number have utilized false documentation to avoid detection while in the United States. The presence of this volume of illegal aliens in the United States impacts heavily on the INS, Department of State and many other Federal, state, county and city agencies.

Passport Frauds

False identification in passport frauds may be divided into two areas of concern: the United States passport and the foreign passport. Either type of passport is readily accepted on an international basis as the travel document for a person's identity and nationality. However, the fraudulent U.S. passport user is primarily implicated with false identification obtained from within the U.S., whereas the fraudulent foreign passport user is primarily implicated with false identification obtained from without the United States.

It is assumed that each United States passport issued is used many times in traveling from country to country as well as entering and departing the U.S. This obviously amounts to many million uses since there are over 10 million valid U.S. passports outstanding.

Summary

A feeling for the distribution of ID fraud by document type and by type of fraud (Alteration, Counterfeit, or Imposter) is given in Table V below. In Table V, the entries are in percent of detected frauds committed. It should be noted that the distribution of fraud shown in Table V most probably reflects the ease with which these frauds can be committed. If, for example, the INS documents were to be made harder to counterfeit, the 29% of presently detected counterfeits might be expected to drop with a corresponding rise in the other categories. Again, it should be emphasized that the data of Table V imply little of the true distribution of frauds since undetected frauds are not included.

TABLE V

User Fraud

	U.S. Passport	NIV	NIV Supporting Documents	IV Supporting Documents	INS Documents
Altered	5%	30%	30%	30%	19%
Counterfeit	0%	20%	60%*	50%*	29%
Imposter	95%	50%	10%	20%	52%

(NIV = non-immigrant visa, IV = immigrant visa)

---

*Includes genuine documents issued by corrupt officials to persons not entitled to them.

INS Documents[1]

Increased investigative activity by INS and liaison with Mexican officials have resulted in the identification throughout Mexico of many well-organized groups engaged in both counterfeiting and altering these Service forms. Criminal prosecution in that country had been sought, however, the 8th Circuit Court in Torreon, Coach., Mexico found that the falsification of United States immigration documents is not a prosecutable offense in that country. Two well-known document falsifiers who had been arrested in the Juarez, Mexico area were released upon that decision. The tribunal ruled that since the issuance of such documents was not authorized by any Mexican authority, there is no Mexican criminal offense for falsification of such documents. One case came about as a result of information furnished to Mexican authorities by a Service investigator. The Baja California Judicial Police arrested three persons at Mexicali and Estacion Delta, Baja, California, Mexico and recovered falsification equipment and a large quantity of blank Forms I-151. It was learned that the more than 200 blank forms recovered were sold to the leader of the group in Guadalajara by two men who were believed to have been arrested and their counterfeiting equipment confiscated in Guadalajara several months earlier.

Also, an intensive investigation by INS and close liaison with Mexican Government officials resulted in the apprehension in Mexico City of the principal counterfeiter of one of the most wide-spread fraudulent document rings ever detected in Mexico. His headquar-

---

[1] All of the following data was taken from INS Intelligence Reports for FY 1973 and 1974.

ters was in Guadalajara where approximately 200 counterfeit Forms I-151 were found in the hands of vendors. Also seized were a small printing press and engraved plates for printing the Forms I-151, selective service cards and an Idaho State Seal, as well as numerous rubber stamps. The counterfeiter had previously been arrested in the United States in 1963 for counterfeiting Forms I-151 and at that time approximately 500 blank counterfeit documents were recovered. He then received a five-year sentence for the 1963 arrest and when last arrested stated that he had spent his entire time in prison perfecting his counterfeiting art.

Among the items seized was a list of the counterfeiter's vendors. There were nine in the State of Jalisco, seven in Guanajuato, three in Micheacan, two in Nuevo Leon and one each in the States of Guerrero, Sinaloa, Sonora and Baja, California, as well as four in Mexico City. There were also twelve vendors listed in the United States: eight in California, and four in Illinois.

The use of altered Forms I-186 by individual imposters and by smugglers to facilitate border crossing by their customers continued to be a popular means of obtaining entry into the United States. Ample supplies of valid Forms I-186 are in the hands of alterers and vendors, who find a ready market for their wares among the thousands of interior Mexicans seeking entry into the United States. As in the case of altered Forms I-151, the workmanship of I-186 alterations has greatly improved over the past few years.

The steady increase over the past few years, except 1974, in the use of unaltered Forms I-151 is, in large part, due to an obvious large supply of forms obtained by vendors from various sources. Some vendors apparently have a large enough supply of documents so that customers may be matched up to forms so closely that it is extremely difficult to detect the fraud. Hopefully, the decline of such cards during 1974 may indicate vendors' supplies are dwindling.

The popularity among imposters of the unaltered Form I-186 as a document to gain entry continues to grow with each passing year. As in the case of the unaltered Form I-151, large supplies in the hands of renters and vendors make it comparatively easy to find a card which matches the imposter.

The problem of Mexican credentials presented by imposters is ever present. It is believed many of these are obtained as favors from Mexican officials. Some are purchased and a few are allegedly found. Many imposters are easily unmasked when interrogation reveals that they are obviously unqualified for the positions they profess to hold. Examples are: illiterate "school teachers," "stenographers" who cannot type, and so on. These documents are used mostly to facilitate entry as an alleged temporary visitor. Although the use of fraudulent Forms I-186 is limited almost exclusively to Mexican nationals and they are predominant in the fraudulent use of the other two Service identity documents, aliens from almost every country employ the use of fraudulent Forms I-151. The following is a common example of this:

Officers of this Service in the New York, New York, area encountered counterfeit Alien Registration Receipt Cards in the possession of illegal aliens. These cards contained the illegal alien's name, photograph, date of birth, and an alien registration number usually found to relate to a file either in the New York district or in another district. The alien in possession of the counterfeit card generally was found to be a visitor or student whose period of temporary stay in the United States had expired. The date of entry on the counterfeit card was invariably found to be the date on which the alien entered the United States for a temporary period. Several natives and citizens of Guyana who had been admitted to the United States on a temporary basis were found to be in possession of such counterfeit cards. Investigation led to the arrest of two sources of these fraudulent documents, one, a Guyanese who had sold the counterfeit cards to aliens of his own nationality after purchasing them from an alien from Columbia. Several of these counterfeit cards were used by Guyanese aliens in an attempt to effect entry into the United States as returning residents and one was used to obtain employment as a teller in a New York City bank. Based upon the testimony of the arrested Colombian alien above and a Guyanese alien who had purchased a counterfeit card directly from him, an indictment was obtained in the United States District Court, for the Southern District of New York, against a third source, a permanent resident alien from Colombia.

Use of fraudulent identity documents supporting a claim to United States citizenship is prevalent among almost every nationality. Fraudulent birth registrations from areas outside the continental United States are also employed. A prime example is the detection of false claims to United States citizenship at ports of entry by aliens presenting counterfeit or fraudulently obtained Puerto Rican birth certificates and United States voter's registration cards. This scheme is commonly used by natives of the Dominican Republic and other Spanish-speaking Latin Americans.

The acquisition of such documents to support a claim to United States citizenship may involve an individual acting alone, or conspiring with others in exchange for monetary gain. Aliens are motivated to enter the United States in this manner for a variety of reasons. An alien's ineligibility to receive a nonimmigrant or an immigrant visa through legitimate State Department channels may be the root cause. Another and more virulent reason may stem from attempts by persons of the criminal classes to gain disguised entry into the United States with contraband or to engage in criminal activities.

For several years there has been widespread use of Puerto Rican birth certificates by aliens to claim United States citizenship.

Generally, the alien is assuming a true identity and has merely purchased a copy of a valid Puerto Rican birth certificate. This has been a particularly favorite practice of Colombian pickpocket rings. Although the Demographic Office in Puerto Rico is supposed to maintain records of when a duplicate birth certificate is issued, investigations by this Service have established that in many instances, particularly when the fraudulent birth-certificate was used to obtain a United States passport, there is no record of any duplicate having been issued. There is an apparently limitless supply of Puerto Rican birth certificates which may be purchased for $30 and up in Puerto Rico and are sold by regular vendors in the Dominican Republic for $50 and up. In one case developed through investigation, it was established that a shoeshine boy, born in 1912, in San Juan, Puerto Rico was selling Puerto Rican birth certificates to Dominicans and Cubans for $40 and up in several instances for an extra fee would assist them in fraudulently obtaining United States passports. Fees for these birth certificates range from $30 to $75.

Many British West Indians, who are allowed to enter Puerto Rico or the United States Virgin Islands without obtaining a nonimmigrant visa, procure fraudulent United States Virgin Islands birth certificates to establish a claim to United States citizenship. These frauds are difficult to detect because of the similarity of race, the fact they all speak the English language and that most of them spend some time in and obtain knowledge of the Virgin Islands before attempting to travel on to the mainland. In the early 1960's, possibly 10% of the British West Indians encountered claim to be United States citizens and a majority of these have some sort of documentation to establish citizenship. The birth certificates are relatively easy and inexpensive to obtain and while many of them relate to true individuals born in the Virgin Islands, the Service is encountering counterfeit certificates which reflect the true name and date of birth of the alien using it.

Since United States citizens need no passports when returning to the United States from Canada or Mexico, nor upon entry into Puerto Rico, the vast majority of United States citizens satisfy the inspectors and are admitted upon a declaration of citizenship. If a doubt arises, proof of citizenship may be required to convince the inspector. While the possibility of false claims always exists, the expertise developed by the immigration officers is invariably difficult to overcome. There are three principal sources available to Service investigators who are engaged in the detection of schemes and violators involving the fraudulent use of Puerto Rican birth certificates and voters' registration cards. The first two sources are concerned with record information -- public and private. Public sources are those of government agencies, Federal, state, county and municipal bodies. Private records are those maintained in the ordinary course of business firms and social agencies not supported by informants. Frauds involving counterfeit non-immigrant visas appear to be conducive to both "ring-type" operation as well as individual activity. The counterfeiting or altering of passports is more conducive to a "ring-type" operation, although a travel agency could well operate in this field at a profit.

Usually, aliens who present these types of documents have been refused issuance of a valid non-immigrant visa because of criminal background, previous deportee history or the American Consul may have had reason to believe that the alien's only purpose in seeking entry into the United States was to work in violation of status. This type of alien then seeks the services of a vendor who usually works hand-in-hand with an unscrupulous travel agency. In such an operation, the cost to the alien may run from several hundred dollars to over a thousand dollars.

There are two common methods by which the fraud rings bring illegal aliens to the United States as imposters with non-immigrant visas. One method is to substitute the pictures affixed to passports containing valid United States B-2 visas, altering birth dates if necessary and renting these altered passports to clients. The other method is to remove the page from a passport which contains a valid United States B-2 visa and sew it into another passport to enable the bearer, fraudulently identified on the title page as the person to whom the valid visa was originally issued, to enter the United States. The second method is the most effective and most difficult to detect inasmuch as the only identifying data on the visa is the name of the person to whom it was issued. Therefore, when a passport is built around this, the name which appears on the visa is used in the passport but the remainder of the identifying data actually relates to the imposter who is using the passport.

The following list reflects the principal types of immigration frauds involving false identification commonly being encountered by INS officers:

1. Personations of United States citizens supported by the following documentation:

    a. Counterfeit, altered and fraudulently obtained United States birth and baptismal certificates;

    b. Altered and fraudulently obtained United States Passports; and

    c. Other counterfeit, altered and fraudulently obtained United States documents of identity i.e., Resident United States Citizen Identification Cards (Form I-179), Social Security Cards, driver's licenses, voter registration cards, etc.

2. Non-immigrant visa frauds:

   a. Counterfeit, altered or fraudulently obtained United States non-immigrant visas;

   b. Altered foreign government passports containing authentic United States non-immigrant visas; and

   c. Counterfeit, altered and fraudulently obtained non-immigrant Border Crossing Cards (Form I-186) and other documents in lieu of non-immigrant visas, i.e., Form I-94, etc.

3. Immigrant visa frauds (including applicants for adjustment of status to that of a lawful permanent resident under Section 245 of the Immigration and Nationality Act):

   a. Personations and fraudulently obtained immigrant visas with valid or fraudulent foreign passports;

   b. Personations, counterfeit and altered Alien Registration Receipt Cards (Form I-151); and

   c. Personations and fraudulently obtained United States birth certificates and baptismal certificates for use in support of relative visa petitions (Form I-130) and Section 245 applications.

The problem of counterfeit, altered or fraudulent identity documents is especially serious in the southwest. In 1967 a total of 4,455 Forms I-151, I-186 and I-179 were detected in that area. Since then overall fraudulent document activity continued at an alarming and increasing rate. The street value of fraudulent documents furnished by vendors actually demonstrated an overall decline in the price of supplied fraudulent documents, which can only be attributed to a high rate of competition among vendors. We must conclude that a high rate of competition in such sales evidences tremendous profit-taking in this criminal endeavor. Comparative figures for Fiscal Years 1967, 1973 and 1974 are as follows:

	I-151 Ctf	I-151 Alt	I-151 Unalt	I-186 Ctf	I-186 Alt	I-186 Unalt	I-179 Ctf	I-179 Alt	I-179 Unalt	TOTAL
FY 67	58	1135	475	0	830	1875	0	69	13	4455
FY 73	3711	1545	2302	904	1410	6536	2	46	31	16487
FY 74	4074	1361	2086	585	1623	6160	6	21	13	15929

Average Price Paid for Documents:

	I-151			I-186			I-179		
	Ctf	Alt	Unalt	Ctf	Alt	Unalt	Ctf	Alt	Unalt
FY 73	$182	$121	$43	$70	$108	$68		$102	$130
FY 74	166	126	80	73	57	40	Unavailable		

False claims to United States citizenship remained relatively static in comparing Fiscal Years 1973 and 1974. There were, during the reporting period, 14,453 false claims to United States citizenship of which 5,010 were documented.

The above statistics reflect a sharp increase in the number of counterfeit Forms I-151 detected in 1974 as compared to 1973. Also, the total number of fraudulent documents detected is higher than in 1973.

There has been much improvement in the quality of both the counterfeit and altered documents over the years, leading to the conclusion that there may be many fraudulent documents which have gone undetected. Increased use of ultra-violet viewing equipment and stepped-up training programs have enabled us to detect the better quality products that may have avoided detection years ago.

The two most common techniques are the counterfeit birth certificate and the IDI method.

1. The counterfeit birth document follows the following process:

    a. The purchase or the production of a counterfeit birth certificate. This is done by photographing the genuine form or the printing of a birth certificate form;

    b. This form is then filled in by the user or the broker for the user; and

    c. This counterfeit is then shown to obtain a genuine driver's license. Those two documents are used to obtain or attempt to obtain a U.S. Passport.

2. The IDI (Infant Death Identity) method, which is becoming more widespread, follows the following pattern:

    a. Search of Vital records, tombstones, newspaper obituaries, morgues to locate the deaths of persons who died in infancy. Infancy in this situation is birth to 5 years;

b. From information obtained in death records, the genuine birth certificate is obtained from the Vital Registrar's Office;

c. The birth certificate is then used to obtain a social security number;

d. The birth certificate and the Social Security number are then used to obtain a driver's license;

e. With these genuine documents, the person applies for a U.S. Passport; and

f. A variation is to use an Identifying Witness rather than a driver's license.

In some cases persons use the birth certificates of deceased adults and follow above procedures to apply for U.S. Passports. This is not too frequent, but it is used.

In the past, affidavits of birth were used along with affidavits of Identifying Witnesses to create false identities. Procedures established by the Passport Office have made it impossible to use this technique.

The IDI method is becoming more prevalent because the documents used are genuine and the fraud is thereby harder to detect.

Another form of fraud technique is to use genuine blank birth certificate forms stolen from Vital Registrar's Office. The blanks are then filled in by the person desiring to assume another identity. In some cases, the blank forms have already been presigned by the Registrar. This same technique is used in the theft of blank driver's licenses.

The alteration of U.S. Passports after issue for use by imposters is accomplished by removing the photograph and replacing it with the photograph of the imposter. In most cases, some official entries regarding age or description are also altered. This practice is exclusively used abroad. It is viable because of the lack of expertise by foreign officials in detecting altered U.S. Passports. The expertise of INS officials generally prohibits this practice for entry into the United States.

False ID "User" Profiles

As reported by the Visa Office, INS, Customs and the Passport Office, users of false ID conform generally to the characteristics shown in Table VI below.

Additional comments indicate a trend for illegally entering aliens to move to the larger urban areas. There is some noted

TABLE VI
FALSE ID USER PROFILES

Document or Activity	Age	Sex	Race or Nationality	Education Level	Criminal Record	Employment Status	Residence in U.S.	Motivation
Visa	18-40	90%M	Central and South American, Caribbean, African, Asian	Some -- Elementary Level	Rare	Unemployed or at low status and pay	Variable	Economic -- to improve standard of living and prospects
INS Documents	18-40	70%M	All	Limited to College Graduate	Generally none	Employed generally	Everywhere but trend toward urban areas	Varied
U.S. Passport	18-40*	78%M	All but predominantly Central and South Americans and U.S. citizens	All. Aliens less than prior citizens	80% have records	Generally employed	All areas	Varied
Narcotics Smuggling	Over 18	75%M	Latin American, European, Asian	Primary Level	Usually	Unemployed or low, menial work	Generally urban areas	Economic -- to make money

*Specific

	Male	Female
Illegal aliens	32	29
Narcotics	29	20
Swindlers	36	26
Fugitives	29	27
Militants	22	23

tendency for political or social unrest in the countries of origin to increase traffic. It is also noted that increasing westernization may be a factor in increasing a tendency to go to the U.S.

There appears no seasonal bias save drug trafficking where holiday and vacation periods are used because of the high load on Customs personnel at these times. Drug traffic is thought also to be affected by the supply and demand situation in its market.

Economic conditions in the U.S. may or may not have an effect on illegal alien traffic since the U.S. economy is invariably better than that of the country of origin.

In general, illegal alien traffic is higher in New York than elsewhere; illicit drug traffic is highest on the West Coast.

SECTION III

SOCIETAL IMPACT AND COSTS

General

The use of false identification to enter or remain illegally in the U.S. by large numbers of aliens has considerable impact on American society. Illegal aliens take jobs that could be held by American citizens or legal resident aliens; they consume welfare services and education funds; they often pay no taxes; they send much of the money that they earn outside the U.S.; they may be exploited by the unscrupulous and the greedy; they are occasionally a factor in crime; they, by their numbers, cause resentment often directed toward all foreign-looking persons, not just illegals; their detection and apprehension and the adjudication of their cases takes considerable time and money. The INS estimates that there are 4-12 million illegal aliens in the U.S. Even a conservative estimate of $100 per week cost to the U.S. in job wages lost, taxes, welfare, and so on yields a staggering annual cost of their presence of $21-62 BILLION.

If even 5%[1] of these illegals have entered the U.S. or remain in the U.S. by using false ID, this cost is in the range of 1 to 3 BILLION per year -- fairly assignable to false ID.

There is, in fact, no total nationwide estimate of the economic impact of the illegal alien on the American taxpayer but their impact on local communities follow as examples.

Welfare Costs

In 1973 the California State Social Welfare Board estimated the cost of welfare payments to illegal aliens to be at least $100 million a year[2].

It was also reported in 1973 that $100 million in welfare funds was paid to illegal aliens in New York City and that 65,000 illegal aliens were attending public schools in that city at a cost of $78 million.

Health Service Costs

In 1974, an $8 million reimbursement claim was received from Los Angeles County for medical expenses incurred by illegal aliens. $3 million was reportedly paid in 1974 to illegal aliens for medical

---

[1] A conservative figure according to the Visa Office.

[2] State of California -- State Social Welfare Board Position Statement, January 1973. Los Angeles Times, 1/27/73.

and hospital expenses by Fresno County, California[1].

Income Tax Losses

Yearly loss, according to a Congressional Report, is $100 million nationwide[2].

A three-month pilot project by INS and IRS produced $168,000 tax collected from 1,700 illegal aliens.

Balance of Payment Losses

Wall Street Journal, September 29, 1971, estimated from $3 to $10 billion sent out of the United States by illegal aliens. In the State of Washington illegal aliens sent out of the United States $7.5 million during the 1974 harvest. A small community post office sent $35 thousand to Mexico in a five-week period[3].

Illegal Aliens Occupy Jobs That Are Attractive to American Citizens

One alien found in Houston was employed at $17,000 per year as a product development engineer. In Maine, an alien was found earning $30,000 a year as a salesman and another earning $900 a month as a computer salesman. In Boston, one was found earning $6.00 per hour as a chemist and another earning $10.00 an hour as a welder. In Providence, two were found earning $8.65 an hour as painters, and in New York City one was found earning $12.00 an hour as a plumber. These are only examples, but it has been estimated that there are more than 1 million illegal aliens occupying well-paid jobs that would be attractive to United States citizens.

CRIMINAL ACTIVITY

Smuggling

A smuggler of narcotics, jewelry, watches, arms and munitions, currency, or any other contraband, needs international mobility to operate effectively. False identification conceals his activity whether he is a principal, controller, or actual carrier of the contraband.

U.S. Customs investigations indicate that false identification is an absolute necessity for a successful international smuggling organization; that false identification is used by smugglers with extensive criminal backgrounds; that false identification conceals

---

[1] Ibid.

[2] New York Times Magazine, 9/16/73. New York Times, 6/12/73.

[3] Investigative Study of the Immigration of Illegal Aliens and Farm Workers in the State of Washington. Study by the State of Washington Interagency Task Force for Agricultural Workers, December 1974.

their criminal backgrounds and provides the organizations with the criminal expertise to evade law enforcement; that, when apprehended, false identification enables these criminals to obtain immediate bail and flee the U.S. before prosecution; that the overall smuggling organization continues to function without any disruption; and that Justice is frustrated until the fugitive can be relocated, apprehended and extradited for prosecution.

A survey conducted by one of the Customs areas involved primarily with the use of false identification in foreign passports disclosed that one of the most prevalent false ID areas of use was that of narcotics smuggling. False identification enables the narcotic smuggler to get into the U.S. as fast as he can with the narcotics, and to get out as fast as he can with the least likelihood of discovery.

In considering the societal impact of drug smuggling the street value of the drugs involved is a conservative measure of the larcenous activity it engenders. It is a conservative measure of the loss of goods and money to society because the fenced value of the goods (the return to the thief) is never close to the true value and generally less than the insurance value. Further, the monies transferred or raised by theft for drugs do not in general return to the economy in the productive way that proceeds of legitimate sales do. They go often to underworld receivers and are used to support other illicit activities which also cost the taxpayer money, decrease his freedom or compound his worry.

As an example, consider a review of arrests, seizures, and narcotic investigations effected by the U.S. Customs Service for the calendar years 1967 through 1974. This survey reveals a total of 416 narcotic seizures valued at $833,849,126 on the illicit street. It also showed that of the total 416 narcotic seizures reported that false identification was used by the smuggler in 143 seizures; that false identification was used by principals, controllers, or other associates connected with the defendant's arrest in 218 narcotic seizures; and that false identification may be involved in 55 narcotic seizures turned over since July 1, 1973, to the Drug Enforcement Administration for their investigation in which a Customs determination could not be made.

Table VII contains the following summaries for Customs cases involving the use of the false identification for narcotic smuggling during the calendar year 1967 through 1974. This data includes the total illicit street level value of $1,672,802,000 for all of the narcotics known through investigation to have been successfully smuggled into the U.S. by these same traffickers or their associates.

TABLE VII.

USE OF FALSE IDENTIFICATION -- NARCOTIC SMUGGLING

CALENDAR YEAR	VALUE OF NARCOTICS SEIZED	VALUE OF KNOWN NARCOTICS SMUGGLED	TOTAL
1967	$ 18,500,000	$ 32,537,500	$ 51,037,500
1968	$ 35,787,000	$ 56,875,000	$ 92,662,000
1969	$ 24,381,492	$ 40,050,000	$ 64,431,492
1970	$ 92,068,750	$ 145,389,500	$ 237,458,250
1971	$296,074,500	$ 384,900,000	$ 680,974,500
1972	$203,899,083	$ 12,350,000	$ 215,249,083
1973	$ 97,257,551	$1,001,700,000	$1,098,957,551
1974	$ 65,880,750		$ 65,880,750
TOTAL	$833,849,126	$1,672,802,000	$2,507,651,126

It should be noted that the Table V data are Customs Service data and accordingly reflect the Federal reorganization of July 1973 which vested investigatory responsibility with the DEA. Customs data following that date reflect only seizures by Customs officials presumably at the point of entry. This accounts largely for the drop in the figures for 1973 and 1974. Any implication that narcotics smuggling declined markedly in 1973 is false.

Of the narcotics seized, about 80% was in the hands of persons utilizing false ID.

It is thought by both DEA and Customs that the extent of drug traffic is closely related to both the economics of the trade and the ready availability of the supply. Seizures are thought to relate directly to the total amount of traffic.

The Passport Office states:

"The use of false identification for the purpose of trafficking in illegal drugs causes almost immeasurable dollar damage to our society as a whole. A person who fraudulently obtains a United States visa for the purpose of bringing illegal drugs into the United States is capable of bringing in, each time he uses that false identity, concentrated hard drugs (cocaine and heroin) which when diluted have a street value of almost a million dollars. For example, during the past two-and-a-half years 206 United States Passports were either applied for or obtained by persons involved in drug activities. The current potential of street value involved by this number of persons is in the neighborhood of 206 million dollars.

The subsequent impact of broken lives and deaths from overdoses of hard drugs brought in by these people is incalculable. This may be expanded to the crimes which drug addicts commit to obtain funds necessary to maintain their drug habit. This has been estimated to run into several hundreds of millions of dollars a year."

FUGITIVES

The impact of a fugitive on society depends to a great extent upon the nature of the criminal offense, the prosecution of which the person is fleeing. The range of such offenses covers all types of felonies. Some of the social impact may be caused by the reoccurence of the offense in a false name plus the ability to escape detection by law enforcement agencies. The dollar impact caused by law enforcement efforts to apprehend a fugitive using a false identity is considerable but impossible to determine with accuracy[1].

Of increasing concern in this context are the militant/radical groups. More traditional fugitive concerns lie with "con" men and espionage agents both of whom use false ID extensively.

The militant/radical impact has a wide scope since these individuals are involved in crimes of violence and terrorist activities. Examples are the Patricia Hearst episode and recent bombing of the State Department. All members of such groups are required to have 3-5 or more different sets of identification documents. One militant went so far as to enlist in the Army to create a false identity.

False ID Investigations & Prosecutions

False ID investigations and prosecutions are mainly the business of the INS, unless a visa fraud is detected overseas in the course of application and insurance. Once an alien is in the U.S., either the Department of Justice, INS, or a state or local authority has jurisdiction. The Customs Service is typically concerned with apprehending smugglers; false ID aspects of a typical Customs case would fall to the jurisdiction of INS. INS activity is discussed below.

INS completed a total of 16,676 investigations of suspected immigration frauds during Fiscal Year 1974. The following statistics indicate the number of Federal criminal violations detected and the sections of Federal law involved.

---
[1] See Appendix A3, Report of the Fugitives Task Force.

	Prosecution Waived by Blanket Waiver	Presented to U.S. Attorney	Thereafter Declined by U.S. Attorney
18 USC 911 False representation as a U.S. citizen	11,373	2,381	2,263
18 USC 1001 False statements	1,347	1,862	1,767
18 USC 1015 False certifications	1	18	4
18 USC 1546 Fraud and misuse of visas and other documents	11,508	2,168	1,877

The Passport Office reports:

During FY 1974 there were 362 fraud cases opened and 341 closed by the Department of State office of Security. During the same period, the Passport Office granted investigative jurisdiction to the FBI in about 50 fraud cases involving matters of primary interest to the organization.

The following table gives figures on criminal prosecutions for passport frauds from July 1, 1973 to February 28, 1975. As of February 28, 1975, there were 136 cases still pending prosecution action.

Criminal Prosecutions

	Opened	Closed	Declined	Dismissed	Convicted	Indicted Fugitive
7-1-73 to 6-30-74	99	89	42	7	19	21
7-1-74 to 2-28-75	40	43	23	2	7	11
TOTAL	139	132	65	9	26	32

Pending

7-1-73	129
2-28-75	136

SECTION IV

COUNTERMEASURES TO CRIMINAL USE OF FALSE ID

General

Detection of an altered passport and non-immigrant visa is, first, visual and subsequently combatted through dissemination of information and intelligence.

Efforts to combat this type of fraud include an exchange of information between INS and the State Department. The interested American consular post is furnished information obtained from the alien relative to the identity of the vendor for transmittal to the foreign government authorities. In addition, new schemes and modus operandi detected through investigation are disseminated to the immigration officers at appropriate ports of entry for their use in identifying such documents during the inspection procedure.

Aliens intercepted at ports of entry or who are encountered after effecting entry with fraudulent passports and/or counterfeit non-immigrant visas have usually been advised by the vendor or travel agent to travel to the United States on weekends, when traffic is at its "peak", in order to escape detection at ports of entry by immigration inspectors. However, vigilant, well-trained immigration inspectors maintain a high detection rate of counterfeit entry documents of all varieties, despite the often overwhelming flow of traffic at ports of entry.

Cases involving fraudulent passports and/or visas are presented to the United States Attorney for criminal prosecution.

The use of false identification by natives of the Philippines has been a problem to the INS for many years. A large number of counterfeit, altered or otherwise fraudulent non-immigrant visas have been presented by imposters from that country. Most of them obtained the documents through unscrupulous travel agents in Manila, who also supply counterfeit airline tickets. Counterfeit non-immigrant visas showing issuance in Manila have been of fairly good quality and difficult to detect. A Philippine national, allegedly connected with a Manila travel bureau, together with an unlicensed travel agent have been identified as the counterfeit visa suppliers. Also, in another case, an employee of another Manila travel bureau supplied a counterfeit visa to an alien after she was denied a visa at the Manila Consulate. He was later arrested for selling a counterfeit airline ticket. A number of cases have been encountered where a visa issued to a person other than the imposter has been utilized. In many of these instances, the imposter's name was similar to that of the person securing the visa. Passports containing the visas may be altered or the visa page may be substituted from one passport to another.

Detection of User Fraud

Considered here are two kinds of entry fraud to be detected with false alien documentation and by a citizen (presumably on illegal business) without a U.S. Passport. They are discussed below:

False Alien Documentation

False Visa Indicators - The following false visa indicators have been noted:

1. The applicant's use of a travel agency to obtain his visa without any appearance at the U.S. Consulate's Office;

2. The quality of the applicant's clothing indicates a lower working class and is not in agreement with his application;

3. The visa applicant is in possession of a foreign passport just recently issued;

4. The visa applicant is in possession of a foreign passport that was issued outside of his native country. Frequently, aliens with criminal records are denied foreign passports in their own country, and they will use their civilian identification cards for travel to an adjacent country to obtain the same passport from a consular office that for the same identification was previously denied to them;

5. The applicant is not a citizen or a resident of the country in which the issuing consulate office is located;

6. The applicant states in his visa application an occupation which does not normally warrant the expense of a trip to the U.S.;

7. The applicant is accompanied by an associate who may or may not be applying for a visa, but is totally familiar with the procedure required for the applicant;

8. The applicant's physical appearance indicates a lower working class than the prestigious title stated for his occupation, i.e., Sanitary Engineer instead of Garbage Man;

9. The applicant states he is married, yet at the same time the purpose of his visit to the U.S. is tourism;

10. The applicant's physical appearance indicates a lower working class but on his application he states his purpose is a tourist and neither his spouse nor his parents are in the U.S.;

11. The applicant's passport shows frequent travel to countries in Europe and South America with very short trips in each country visited;

12. The applicant states in his application an intended departure that is immediate;

13. The applicant omits to answer the visa question "What address do you wish your visa be mailed to?"; and

14. The applicant's language proficiency is not in agreement with his foreign passport identity and nationality.

False Entry Without a U.S. Passport

The U.S. Customs Service finds that the smuggler continually seeks new ways to enter the U.S. with false identification. The following method is also frequently utilized by the U.S. citizen.

The subject assumes an alias and then obtains the following credentials for the purpose of identification:

1. State driver's license;

2. Bank card and account;

3. Library card;

4. Social Security card;

5. Voter identification card; and

6. Various club membership I.D. cards.

Armed with the above credentials and falsely obtained U.S. Passport, the subject purchases a ticket to leave the United States for his destination. Upon arriving at his destination, the foreign entry is easily accomplished since a U.S. Passport makes entry into most foreign countries an easy matter.

In order to gain easy access back into the United States without a passport, the subject then purchases a ticket in the assumed name and returns to the U.S. via Nassau, Jamaica or other various locations from which the U.S. Immigration Service allows entry into

the U.S. with the showing of any of the credentials in the absence
of a U.S. Passport.

This method of entry evades detection by Federal law enforcement agencies and also enables the subject to keep his U.S. Passport
clean of any entry stamps that would reveal his return to the U.S.

Application Phase

Visa Office

One of the most effective countermeasures that the Visa Office
has used and continues to use against fraud is encouragement of
alertness among consular officers abroad. An attempt is made to
remind visa issuing officers that the incentives to gain entry to
the U.S. are great, to point out techniques often used, to call
attention to unusual trends in visa issuance at particular posts
and to offer other support as needed.

Working with the Immigration and Naturalization Service, an
attempt is being made to standardize certain forms that prospective
providers of financial support and prospective employers are expected to file. The problem of false labor certifications is being
attacked with the Department of Labor. But, since most of the
documents submitted in the application phase are of foreign origin,
control over them is limited and individual officer alertness is
the most effective weapon.

INS

The most effective countermeasures to combat the "application"
phase of fraud is the training of all Service officers to increase
their sensitivity to frauds. This is done through a formal training
program at the Service Academy in Port Isabel, Texas, and also at
local training sessions. Close cooperation at all levels with the
Department of State and the Department of Labor are stressed.

Considerable success has also resulted from the following
described Suspect Third Party Program.

The Service has always been concerned with the problem of combatting frauds engaged in by aliens in connection with attempts
made to unlawfully effect entry and remain in the United States.
In 1963, an increase was noted in the activity of unscrupulous
individuals involved as third parties in the preparation and submission of visa petitions and other applications to the Service.
These include applications for extension of temporary stay of non-
immigrant visitors, change of status from one category of non-
immigrant to another non-immigrant status and adjustment of status
from a non-immigrant status to that of a permanent resident in the
United States. The third parties take undue advantage of people
who desire to do everything possible to aid in the immigration of

relatives and friends and frequently engage in fraud, misrepresentation, furnishing false identity documents and other irregularities.

It has been the practice of some unscrupulous attorneys, travel agents, notaries public, employment agents and so-called "immigration consultants" to arrange marriages of convenience to assist aliens to obtain permanent residence in this country. If they are unable to locate a United States citizen to marry an alien for a fee, they often will supply an alien with false documentation as a citizen to go through the ceremony and file the necessary visa petition. There is an increasing trend of United States citizens to engage in multiple marriages for the purpose, using birth certificates or identity documents of various United States citizens. In furtherance of Service efforts to combat such unethical and unlawful practices and to aid in the identification and detection of the individuals concerned, the Suspect Third Party Program was initiated on November 4, 1963. Operating procedures, which included a vigorous prosecution policy, were established and field offices were directed to follow them closely. Many of the investigations under this program disclosed criminal violations, including aliens and other persons who for substantial fees assisted them in their efforts to evade quota and other restrictions embodied in the immigration laws. The criminal statutes violated were 18 USC 371 (conspiracy), 18 USC 1001 (false statements) and 18 USC 1546 (fraud).

Passport Office

The most effective countermeasures to combat the "application" phase of fraud is the training of all officers to increase their ability to recognize frauds. This is done at fraud training seminars at our field Passport agencies as well as in Washington. In connection with these specialized seminars, conducted training seminars have been conducted for interested outside agencies in field areas. Representatives from the following agencies have attended these specialized seminars: FBI, DEA, FAA, Postal Service, Customs, Office of Security of the Department of State (SY) and INS.

Special seminars have been conducted by invitation to Customs officers and INS officers.

Fraud seminars are now being conducted for Postal and Clerk of Court Personnel who accept passport applications in the U.S.

Use Phase

Visa Office

Presentation of counterfeit immigrant visas for admission to the U.S. is virtually unknown. All the identity fraud appears to be in the application phase.

For the non-immigrant visa, reliance is primarily on the alertness of the INS primary inspectors at ports of entry to spot photo substitutions, page switching, or visa altering. Efforts to counter the attempted use of counterfeit visas include standardization of the visa plate, improvement of the special features of the ribbon, notation of visa refusals on passports, maintenance of a visa lookout system, and introduction of the counterfoil in high fraud areas. The counterfoil is a peel-off, paste-in paper wafer with a number and a finely printed design on it. The visa is printed in the passport partially over this wafer. Although attempts to counterfeit the1 ounterfoil have surfaced (after a year of apparently trouble-free use), it is believed that it has been a useful addition in high fraud areas and has deterred some counterfeiters.

It should be pointed out that measures such as these may deter certain uses of false identification, but encourage other methods of circumventing the law -- false claims to American citizenship and increased efforts to enter the U.S. without visas and thus without inspection are likely to emerge.

One of the most promising recent steps in the area of countering the use of false identification is a joint project being carried out by the Visa Office and the Immigration and Naturalization Service with the advice and assistance of a private consulting firm to develop fraud-proof non-immigrant visas and alien registration cards. Pilot tests of the recommended new system of non-immigrant visa issuance and control are to begin shortly.

INS

Again it is believed that education of Service officers is the most effective weapon to combat "use" frauds. INS officers must be adept at spotting photo substitution, page switching, visa altering, impersonations, etc. All officers also have available to them ultraviolet light equipment, including portable types for use in the field. Close cooperation between the Department of State consular officers and INS officers has proven effective. Suspect documents are checked by telephone to determine if they were issued by consular officers.

The Service's Fraudulent Document Center was established in 1958 to develop measures to combat false claims to United States citizenship by Mexican aliens using fraudulent documents. The Center furnishes information to assist Service officers in conducting investigations and obtaining evidence, compiles statistics to determine the scope of the problem and assembles and coordinates information pertaining to Mexican false claimants by indexing known and suspected violators as well as the fraudulent documents. The Chief Patrol Agent, Yuma, Arizona, has overall responsibility for the Fraudulent Document Center; 5,924 cases were added to the files during the Fiscal Year bringing the total number of files at

the facility to almost 50,000. Service officers and officials of
other agencies directed 6,128 inquiries to the facility for record
checks in Fiscal Year 1974. One out of four of the inquiries resulted in the location of prior records relating to documented
false claims to citizenship. The information available from the
files proved invaluable in determination of the citizenship status
of those attempting to perpetrate frauds.

Customs Service

The most effective countermeasure to false identification is
the proper training of front-line personnel to alert them to profiles, methods of use, and other intelligence available concerning
unusual techniques used by narcotic smugglers. In addition, close
cooperation is stressed with the State Department, and the Immigration Service relative to ongoing investigations, so that all levels
of the entry screening process can be fully aware of current trends
and provide greater efficiency.

SECTION V

RECOMMENDATIONS FOR AMELIORATION OF THE FALSE ID PROBLEM

General

This section sets forth the preliminary recommendations of the Task Force on Federal Documents for the substantial decrease and eventual elimination of the False ID Problem as a practical matter. The recommendations are intended both to make abuse of federal documents more difficult and to engender easier, surer, and more efficient detection of frauds perpetrated with false documents. It is understood that the issues involved here are, to some extent, international in character and that effective solutions will often require multi-national agreements and cooperation.

International Agreements

It is recommended that the Departments of Justice and State utilize their resources to obtain international acceptance of standards and uniform guidelines for passport control. The standards and guidelines should include consideration of issuance requirements, in general, ID required particularly, printing, photography and counterfeit, alteration and imposter countermeasures.

The acceptance of uniform guidelines of this sort would be an important step in the establishment of International Passport controls, a requisite for efficient address to the international false ID problem.

Such a program could be initiated as one of the law enforcement programs of Interpol and the International Association of Chiefs of Police. These two organizations have worldwide representation and are natural channels abroad. An international anti-fraud training program could be a part of a joint program.

Domestic Practices

Prosecution of Cases

It is recommended that guidelines be issued by the Department of Justice to all of their U.S. attorneys concerning the magnitude and importance of the false identification problem. This may provide a greater acceptance by the U.S. attroneys for the prosecution of selective cases involving false passports, non-immigrant visas, and Customs Baggage Declarations, particularly in narcotic smuggling.

In previous cases effected by the U.S. Customs Service, Assistant U.S. Attorneys have been reluctant to include these additional charges against the defendant. They felt it was superfluous; that it did not warrant the time and effort; and that the primary charge of narcotic smuggling was sufficient. However, these additional counts insure a prosecutor's chances to obtain a conviction, especially with an uncooperative defendant implicated in a narcotic smuggling conspiracy. Finally, principals, controllers and their associates who use false identification to enter the U.S. become highly vulnerable to Federal prosecution.

Inter-Agency Cooperation

The desirability of more intensive cooperation among the various agencies, bureaus, offices and departments having an interest in the false ID problem has been noted. There are several ways of effecting this and degrees of formality which might properly attach to these activities. They range from informal joint seminars on aspects of the problem such as have been conducted with success in the past, to the establishment of a national fraudulent document center patterned somewhat after the successful INS center at Yuma, but focused on the common needs of the member community.

In this vein, suggestions have been advanced concerning the establishment of "banks" to centralize state data such as Driver's License information, birth and death records and the like, from those states which have computerized or otherwise regularized their vital records activities.

Interstate Activities

Abuse of the birth certificate and driver's licenses through their uses as breeder documents impacts federal document control of concern to this Task Force. Accordingly, it is recommended that the states, singly or jointly, move to eliminate the IDI syndrome and better control both the birth certificate and the driver's license. Nevada law S.B. 391 (Attachment II of this report) is cited as a model in this regard.

At the very least, states should agree on a standard birth certificate form, materials and methods. The availability of facsimile documents should be prescribed and the use of legitimate forms controlled.

Training and Education

Extensive and intensive use of training programs for all officials having any connection with the false ID problem is recommended. Such training should be reviewed and updated as appropriate.

Legislation

Loopholes in existing legislation[1] have been noted from time to time which are not in the interest of society and every effort should be made to close them expeditiously.

---

[1] Section 1546 of 18 USC relating to the possession of a fraudulent Alien Registration Receipt Card.

REPORT OF THE STATE AND LOCAL IDENTIFICATION DOCUMENTS TASK FORCE

ON THE

SCOPE OF THE FALSE IDENTIFICATION PROBLEM AND

PRELIMINARY RECOMMENDATIONS FOR SOLUTIONS

Submitted to

Federal Advisory Committee On False Identification
David J. Muchow, Chairman

May 1976

CONTENTS

SECTION I — INTRODUCTION 173
    Purpose 173
    Scope 173
    Data Gathering 174
    Evaluation of Data 175

SECTION II — THE FALSE ID PROBLEM 177
    Application Phase 177
    Application Patterns 179
    Use Phase 179
    Intended and Common Usage 179
    Fraudulent Uses 179
    Document Fraud 180
    Counterfeit Documents 180
    Altered Documents 180
    False ID Users 181
    False ID Victims 182

SECTION III — COUNTERMEASURES TO CRIMINAL USE OF FALSE ID 183
    Countermeasures Presently Employed 183
    Application Phase 183
    Birth Certificates 183
    Motor Vehicle Operator's Permits 184
    "Use" Phase 185

SECTION IV — RECOMMENDATIONS 186
    Birth Certificate 186
    Driver's Licenses 188
    Other Comments 189

Report of the State and Local Documents Task Force

on the

Scope of the False Identification Problem

Recommendations for Solutions

SECTION I

INTRODUCTION

Purpose

The State and Local Documents Task Force was to study the state and local documents commonly utilized in establishing false identities; to establish false identity use patterns for the subject documents; and to suggest practical solutions to this abuse.

Scope

While there are many documents which originate at a state or local office, it was determined as a result of survey, that the most frequently used documents for establishing false identities are the birth certificate and the driver's license. Therefore, the Task Force expended the bulk of its effort on studying the false identity problem as it relates to these important documents.

It is a fair statement that the potential use of the birth certificate as a "breeder" of other false documents and the universal acceptance of the driver's license as valid ID makes these two documents essential to the establishment of a full false identity. While a variety of imaginative frauds can be used to generate false identity documents, the possession of these two assuredly makes the process easier and the likelihood of apprehension less.

These two documents are similar in that both are issued by states under state control. There are no federal regulations relating to the issuance of either document.

The work of the Task Force was accordingly very broad in scope because there are more than fifty states and territories of interest with significant differences in procedures and standards. It was necessary to collect data from all the states to completely delineate the problem. Even greater breadth was added by the fact that driver's licenses and copies of birth certificates may be issued within states and territories through scattered local offices. There are, for example, over 7,000 offices in the country authorized to issue certified copies of birth certificates. Because of the large numbers of issuing offices, procedures may, and often do vary from area to area within a state. Accordingly, statements made here relating to the system for issuance of birth certificate copies or for the issuance of drivers' licenses are representative common practice but do not necessarily reflect the procedures in every state or even in every part of a single state.

Data Gathering

Data was acquired through surveys and from existing reports and interviews. Task Force surveys are described as follows:

1. One survey questionnaire was sent to all fifty states and eight independent cities and territorial Vital Registration officials. The purpose of the survey was to secure information on the matching of infant death records to the corresponding birth certificates. The survey also requested the number of offices in each area that issue copies of vital records and solicited suggestions for reducing fraud in birth certificate issuance. All fifty-eight registration areas* responded.

2. A letter was also sent by Dr. E. B. Perrin (Director, National Center for Health Statistics) and Mr. Clarence M. Kelley (Director, Federal Bureau of Investigation) to each state and territorial health officer. The letter announced the formation of the Federal Advisory Committee on False Identification (FACFI), requested suggestions that would help to reduce the fraud problem as it relates to vital records, and enlisted their support for the work of the FACFI. Fifty-eight letters were sent and twenty-six responses were received.

3. A survey was made of all state and provincial motor vehicle administrators and chiefs of enforcement by the American Association of Motor Vehicle Administrators to secure information on the automobile operator's license problem in false identification. One hundred and sixty questionnaires were mailed out and thirty-three responses were received.

4. A survey was conducted among the Department of Motor Vehicle District Directors in New York State by the Director of the Department of Motor Vehicles. This survey attempted to gather information regarding the extent of the false identity problem as it exists in New York State; a profile of those obtaining

---

*Fifty states and Washington, D.C., N.Y. City, Puerto Rico, American Samoa, Guam, Panama Canal Zone, Virgin Islands, Trust Territory of the Pacific Islands.

false driver's licenses; and recommendations for reducing the problem. The survey was sent to thirteen District Directors; all replied.

5. Data was also obtained from the Passport Office (PPO) and the Immigration and Naturalization Service (INS) regarding the extent of use of the birth certificate and operator's license in their operations. An estimate of the extent of fraud involved in the use of vital records and operator's licenses in matters of concern to INS and PPO was also obtained. The Passport Office additionally constructed a general profile of persons obtaining passports fraudulently.

Evaluation of Data

The total volume of fraudulent use, falsification, and counterfeiting of the birth certificate and operator's licenses is unknown for two reasons: first, because of the difficulties in detecting such use and, second because there is apparent inadequate reporting of those cases which are detected. The data available, however, though spotty and not precise, do suggest a problem of some magnitude. For example, the Yuma Fraudulent Document Center reported that at least 5,500 false fraudulent applications for U.S. entry certification are made annually.

More and reliable data is obviously needed to fully delineate the fraudulently obtained driver's licenses and birth certificates for criminal activities. Data is particularly sparse in estimating the number of times persons apprehended for other crimes are found to have false identification documents in their possession, a lack which would seem to be easily rectified by the application of uniform reporting standards.

A common method of establishing a false identity has surfaced, however, and its use is considered widespread by law enforcement officials although hard data have not been obtained. This method is known as the "Infant Death Identity" (IDI) Syndrome and is described as follows:

1. Through public sources, death records, tombstones, newspaper "morgues" and the like, an infant who died young is located who had about the same birthdate and sex of an individual seeking to establish a false identity.

2. The false identity seeker requests (sometimes by telegram) a certified copy of the dead infant's birth certificate. The fact of death is rarely noted on the birth certificate; birth and death records sections are commonly separate.

3. Using the birth certificate as his own, the individual acquires a driver's license, passport or whatever other credential can be so acquired.

4. The addition of a Social Security Registration card, bank accounts, credit accounts, and so on are now undertaken -- all legitimate and all based on the original fraudulent birth certificate.

That this method works quite well is beyond dispute. Cases are recorded by the Passport Office, the INS and the U.S. Customs Office documenting the widespread use and efficiency of the Infant Death Identity (IDI) Syndrome.

The social significance of this technique should not be underestimated since its use appears to be particularly common among drug traffickers, who require several alternate identities and passports for their activities[1]. The use of IDI techniques by fugitives of one kind or another is verified by law enforcement officers across the country.

Directions for application of the IDI technique are given in exquisite detail in a current and popular "underground" book[2], and are commonly quoted in underground newspapers and other "specialty" publications. The Paper Trip, in fact, advises against document theft and impersonation as a means of establishing identity since it is easier, surer and less risky to use the IDI method.

Cases have been reported to the Task Force in which fugitives have been apprehended with several complete sets of false identity documents in their possession - all apparently obtained by IDI methods.

Because they may be related to Welfare fraud and the IDI syndrome, additional investigation is thought warranted concerning the criminal use of marriage and death records. At this time, no hard data whatever are available relative to the abuse of these two records types. It is inferentially concluded that death records were sometimes used in establishing an IDI credential but it is noted that there are many public sources of death information (tombstones, for example) besides vital records data.

The data available suggest that a false ID potential of some magnitude exists for these two primary state and local documents. A fuller and more quantitative description of the problem is given in the following sections of this report.

---

[1] The Passport Office has discovered several IDI cases wherein an individual with an IDI obtained passport served as affiant for several others in obtaining their passports.

[2] The Paper Trip, publisher unknown, undated.

SECTION II

THE FALSE ID PROBLEM

Of major concern is the abuse of the birth certificate and the driver's license, represented by the use of these documents to establish false identities. Both (particularly the birth certificate) are breeder documents, and both are important aids to the commission of crimes where a false identity is necessary for the criminal activity.

These documents can be either altered, counterfeited or used as the basis of an IDI process as previously described. The main thrust of this investigation was the fraudulent acquisition of valid documents, though alteration and counterfeiting are discussed also.

That this is an important matter is attested by the following statement by FBI Director, Clarence Kelley:

> "During the course of recent FBI invesitgations, positive information has been developed which clearly indicates that subversive and criminal subjects are resorting to the use of counterfeit identification documents, as well as authentic documents of other persons in order to carry out their illegal endeavors. These criminal activities include narcotics, illegal immigration, insurance frauds, counterfeit checks, passport fraud, auto theft and many other crimes."

The problem for state and local authorities is to maintain a cost effective procedure for legitimate birth certificate and driver's license issuance while preventing illegal issuances and detecting the use of counterfeit documents.

The false ID problem can, in the context of this report, be broken down into two independent processes or phases. They are the "application" phase, in which a state or local agency is requested to supply a document (birth certificate or driver's license), and the "use" phase, in which the holder of the document displays it as proof of identity in the conduct of a transaction of one sort or another. These two phases are explored in more detail below.

Application Phase

Birth Certificate: Application for a certified copy of a birth certificate normally requires the submission of a written request to the appropriate state or local vital records office, providing information necessary to locate the birth certificate. Ordinarily, the information required consists of the name of the individual whose birth the certificate attests, the date and place of the birth, and the names of the parents. A fee is also required and this must be presented prior to issuance of the copy. Some copies are issued to applicants "in person," but these represent only about 20% of the total copies issued. No identification is usually required to obtain certified copies of birth certificates because of the high volume of requests and the fact that over 80% are requested by mail or by telegram.

Motor Vehicle Operator's License: Application for a motor vehicle operator's license must be made in person to an authorized official. Applicants must establish (usually with a birth certificate), that they meet the minimum age requirements, provide proof of driving ability, demonstrate knowledge of traffic laws, and adequately satisfy certain health requirements. The birth certificate is commonly accepted as proof of identity as well as age for driver's license application purposes. For interstate transfer of licenses, the old license itself is ordinarily the only ID required. Other or additional documents may be required to establish identity of the applicant. The usual documents accepted for identification, besides the birth certificate, are a social security card, driver's license from another state, military ID, U.S. Passport, or a foreign country's driver's license.

Non-driver's Identity Card: Thirty-four states have instituted issuance of a non-driver's identification card, the appearance of which is similar to the driver's license and which is issued by the same officials. The need for such a document derives from the widespread use of the driver's license for identification in check cashing and for other face-to-face business transactions.

Some form of identification is required before issuance of this card, but the requirements appear to be minimal. Usually the same types of documents required for a driver's license are required for this document. None of the documents presented for identification for the issuance of either a driver's license or a non-driver's license are verified prior to the issuance of the non-driver's ID.

The estimated number of applications for these documents is:

Document	No. of Applications Per Year
Birth Certificate (copies)	8 to 10 million
Driver's License	12 million
Non-Driver's ID Card	Unknown

It is not possible to estimate with surety the number of applications per year which are fraudulent. Certain figures are available, however, which are suggestive of a significant problem. The U.S. Immigration and Naturalization Service (INS) estimates that in 1974, for example, about 5100 of the birth certificates submitted to it were fraudulent - and the number is rising. Similar estimates from the Passport Office (PPO) suggest that their <u>discovery</u> of false birth certificates and driver's licenses was about 500 in 1974[1], up 25% over 1973.

Application Patterns

The Washington, D.C. registry reports that birth certificate requests for foreign travel and school admission show seasonal variations while job and social security related requests remain constant. <u>Almost half the applications for birth certificates which were examined by the D.C. Registry stated vague reasons for their requests.</u>

Use Phase

Intended and Common Usage

Each document is used in the following ways.

Birth Certificate: Used to establish age, citizenship, and parentage of the individual to whom the certificate pertains. The establishment of these facts are necessary for school entrance, to secure employment, to obtain a passport, to claim social security benefits, and for other commercial or business purposes where one or all of these facts must be verified. The total utilization of the birth certificate as a means of establishing the identity of the bearer is impossible to estimate.

Driver's License: Issued as an authorization to operate a motor vehicle. In the last several years, however, it has become the single most sought and accepted means of identification. Merchants accept it for identification in cashing checks or to validate the use of credit cards.

Non-driver's Identification Card: Intended as a means of identification for the cashing of checks, use of credit cards, and other instances where proof of ID is required; for all uses of a driver's license except the operation of a motor vehicle.

Fraudulent Uses

Complete information regarding the use of fraudulent or improperly obtained birth certificates for each of these purposes is not available. As noted, however, their use as false ID is thought considerable based on fragmentary and inferential data.

Substantiating ID is sometimes requested at "use points" but this is ordinarily a secondary matter, however. The Passport Office, for instance, requires documents to identify the individual in addition to a birth certificate which establishes citizenship. These

---

[1] Of about 2.5 million passports applied for.

additional documents would include driver's licenses, Social Security cards, military or industrial ID. However, in the majority of situations in which the birth certificate or the driver's license are used as primary ID, no additional documentation is required.

When a driver's license or non-driver's ID card is used for check cashing or using a credit card, other identification may or may not be required. In the majority of cases it is not.

Document Fraud

Counterfeit Documents

Counterfeit birth certificates and driver's licenses are used extensively in the establishment of false ID. Such documents are apparently available from many sources and the methods used to create them are varied. One method which has been utilized is to obtain a valid document, either driver's license or certified copy of a birth certificate, and blank out the information to be changed. Once this is done, the form can be reproduced still showing the signature of the official who issued the document and other information that should be retained and the new information is then entered on the document. This procedure produces a document which looks like a valid document and detection of the fraud is difficult.

Other methods used in counterfeiting documents include stealing of actual forms or printing false forms. When presented to untrained, uninformed persons these counterfeit documents may be, and often are, accepted without question as being authentic. With birth certificates, the counterfeit propensity is especially large for the following reasons: there are over 7000 local and state offices issuing birth certificates under their own laws and regulations. No federal control or unifying guidelines exist. The result is the issuance of hundreds of different sizes, shapes, and formats used for these documents. It is accordingly difficult for a document inspector to learn all the legal forms and recognize a counterfeit. Many certificates are issued on ordinary paper making counterfeiting and tampering with legitimate certificates easy for the experienced criminal or the clever amateur.

Altered Documents

Alterations of birth certificates or driver's licenses, while it does occur, appears to be a minor problem compared to counterfeiting or impersonation. The probable reason for this is that alterations are often detectable and are likely to raise questions. From surveys of motor vehicle registries in the state of New York and by the American Association of Motor Vehicle Administration (AAMVA), for example, it appears that the distribution of types of ID document frauds are typically:

	NYS	AAMVA
Altered	3%	80%
Counterfeit	36%	10%
Imposter	61%	10%

The large number of detected "altered" documents in the AAMVA study may be due to the fact that alterations are easier to spot. It is impossible to know how many counterfeits and imposters escaped. The most frequent use of the alterations is thought to be by persons wanting to appear older (to drink or to marry).

False ID Users

It is difficult to develop a profile of those using birth certificates and driver's licenses in establishing false identification. This may in itself suggest that no real pattern exists. Most of the persons and organizations affected by users of false identities do not collect information of this type. The Passport Office, however, was able to provide some partial information relative to passport fraud. It is:

>Age - 18 to 26 years,
>Sex - male more often than female,
>Race - not available,
>Education - not available,
>Employment Status - unknown,
>Residence (rural, urban) - unknown, and
>Prior criminal record - not available.

The Passport Office indicates that the persons obtaining passports illegally fall into the following categories of criminal activity. These categories include: illegal aliens, narcotic dealers, fugitives, members of radical groups, espionage agents, confidence men and others.

Other data relating to false identity "use" is also minimal because of the lack of records.

Regarding variations of false identity use with geographical areas, the Passport Office also reports that most passport frauds are perpetrated in New York City and Los Angeles. The birth certificates used in passport fraud originate in many places, the most prevalent being California but many counterfeit documents have also been encountered in Illinois, primarily in Chicago. The Immigration and Naturalization Service experience is that the southwest and New York City appear to be the primary areas for illegal aliens. Their means of entry is from Mexico into the southwest or from the Caribbean through the Virgin Islands or Puerto Rico into New York City. Most have false identification, mainly birth certificates, obtained in Mexico, the Virgin Islands, Puerto Rico or in one or another of the Caribbean Islands.

No information is available to the Task Force to indicate whether false identity "use" activity varies with season of year but the economic climate appears to have some effect. There is a definite increase in alien traffic at times when economic conditions in neighboring countries are poor.

False ID Victims

The Task Force was able to obtain very little data from which to draw a profile of victims of the use of false identities. Everyone who is in any way affected by the criminal activity of someone utilizing false identity is, in a sense, a victim. This would include victims of confidence men; anyone addicted to narcotics; any business establishment that is defrauded; any unemployed citizen who cannot find work because of illegal aliens filling available jobs; and the general taxpaying public.

Birth registries and motor vehicle bureaus receive little feedback on the social, psychological, political or other costs of false ID. Some of the social or psychological impact of false identification is indicated about victims by the above statement. The INS estimates that a significant number of illegal aliens hold jobs that might otherwise be filled by unemployed citizens or acquire unemployment benefits supported by the taxpayers.

False identification investigations, prosecutions, and declinations reported by the Passport Office for the year 1974 included 553 domestic and 238 foreign fraud cases completed with 99 criminal prosecutions closed. The Immigration and Naturalization Service apprehended 14,000 Mexicans fraudulently claiming U.S. Citizenship (5,000 were documented claims with most having valid birth certificates). No information was provided in regard to the number of prosecutions.

Total estimated costs or societal impact of the use of false identity cannot be estimated from information available to the Task Force. No cost information was available from either the INS or the Passport Office.

SECTION III

COUNTERMEASURES TO CRIMINAL USE OF FALSE ID

In this section the subject of countermeasures to creation and use of false identities is discussed. Those countermeasures now employed or about to be employed are described first, and following that, preliminary recommendations for additional countermeasures are given.

COUNTERMEASURES PRESENTLY EMPLOYED

The discussion of current countermeasures is divided by the "application" and "use" phase and by the two types of documents, birth certificates and motor vehicle operator's permits.

Application Phase

Birth Certificates

Matching of birth and infant death records: It is sometimes possible to detect birth certificate requests for a person who died before the age of one, because some states match the birth and death records and post the fact of death on the birth certificate. For those who die after the first year, there is no consistently used method at present which indicates the fact of death in the registry of births. Also, the infant death matching program is normally only carried out at the state Vital Records Office, and if the certified copy is requested from a local Vital Records Office, detection would not be possible, the information not being available to the local registry. This program has minimal impact in reducing fraudulent use of the birth record nationally since all states do not have such a program. Even in those states that do match, very few have a matching program in the local Vital Records Office. The effectiveness of the program even if broadly implemented may be short term because counterfeits could replace fraudulent applications of deceased persons.

Keeping track of the number of applications for particular birth certificates: Again this program has a minor impact on reducing the fraudulent use of birth certificates because of the small number of states doing it and the very few improper applications which could probably be detected in this manner.

Use of safety paper to prevent alteration of valid certified copies: Several states use safety paper which makes alterations obvious. If generally used, it would be harder to produce a passable counterfeit.

Motor Vehicle Operator's Permits

The National Highway Traffic Safety Administration (NHTSA) Highway Safety Program Standard No. 5, Driver Licensing, requires the states to seek positive proof of full name, date, and place of birth prior to issuance of an initial driver's license. Currently, 41 states claim to comply with this provision. This program is probably effective in dealing with persons in the 16 to 18 age range. These people probably have had driver's education in high school and the driver education certificate along with the birth certificate should identify the individual effectively. For persons applying for their first license at a later age, it becomes more difficult to confirm identity. Normally, a birth certificate is presented and this is accepted as proof of both age and identity.

The National Driver Register is designed to assist states in problems of interstate driver control: States participate on a voluntary basis, entering in the Register the names of drivers who have had their licenses suspended; and requesting a search of the Register files for records of applications prior to issuance of new licenses to those persons newly arrived in the state. The impact of this program on the false ID problem is expected to be minimal since its purpose and design is only to prevent persons with a suspended license in one state from going to another state and getting a license.

Another interstate control of licensed drivers available to the states is the Driver License Compact: Twenty-nine states are now members of the Compact. The Compact requires the member states to forward records of out-of-state traffic violation convictions to the driver records agency in the home state of the driver, and upon issuance of a driver license in any state it requires all previous current valid licenses to be surrendered to the new state of issuance.

Additionally, Section 6-101 (c) of the Uniform Vehicle Code (UVC), a model traffic code available to the states and endorsed by NHTSA, provides that out-of-state drivers surrender all licenses held by the applicant upon issuance of a new license, and that such licenses be returned to the issuing state. Twenty-nine states belong to the Compact and eight additional states have the UVC provision. However, not all of these states adhere to the provisions of either the Compact or the statute.

Twenty-eight states now have licenses which they consider tamper proof. However, since alteration of licenses represents a small percentage of the total false ID problem, the impact in this area is limited. It would be advantageous, however, if all states were to develop such a program since it would aid in eliminating this portion of the problem. It would also make it more difficult to develop counterfeit licenses. Also, 36 states now have photos on their licenses which also aids in reducing the possibility of alteration and makes counterfeiting more difficult.

Use Phase

For the most part, countermeasures at the point of use are almost non-existent. The only organization found with an extensive program for investigating evidence presented is the Passport Office. Through a training program, PPO clerks have been sensitized to fraudulent practices. Accordingly, when confronted with suspicious documents, a verification of them is attempted. This procedure is principally responsible for the detection of passport frauds.

In the commercial sector, many businessmen do not examine a driver's license closely when it is presented for the cashing of a check. It is fair to conclude, therefore, that very few countermeasures are applied in the "Use" phase. Most detection of false ID occurs after the commission of a fraud.

SECTION IV

RECOMMENDATIONS

This section sets forth the recommendations of the Task Force for countering the false ID problem. Because of fundamental differences in the documents themselves, the methods for obtaining them, the standardization and control applied to their distribution and their differential viability in the conduct of frauds and other criminal activity, the recommended actions are grouped by document.

These recommendations derive not only from deliberations of the Task Force and examination of data and evidence made available to it; but also from careful consideration of the suggestions offered by officials in the field. Many of the suggestions represent the common thinking of many individuals considering the issues independently.

Birth Certificate

1. Match all deaths to the corresponding birth certificate. This would represent an extension of the infant death matching program. The cost of such a program would be very high because of the time required to manually match the records as well as the need to send copies of death certificates to other states when the birth and death do not occur in the same state. If this program was instituted, and if information was transmitted to the local Vital Records Offices, it would be an effective means of preventing persons from using a deceased person's birth record. The IDI syndrome would largely disappear.

2. Establish better lines of communication between the states and Federal Agencies. This would be a very helpful and inexpensive mechanism of dealing with the fraudulent ID problem. Many states have noted that while they cooperate with the Passport Office, INS, the FBI and other Federal Agencies, they are never informed of the outcome of cases on which they have been consulted. The states are not routinely notified when someone who is apprehended bears an improper birth certificate obtained from their state.

3. Increase the penalty provisions of the vital statistics law with regard to the possession and use of counterfeit, altered, or imposter certificates. This proposal is being given strong consideration now, and several states are already in the process of strengthening their laws. Also, the Model State Vital Statistics Act, model legislation recommended by HEW, is presently being revised and stronger penalty provisions are being considered for

inclusion. This may have some effect on the use of false ID for relatively trivial offenses.

4. Vital records offices keep record of requests for certified copies. Often the same birth record is multiply used to establish false identities. If records are kept of the certified copy requests for each record, the possibility of false ID use would be raised and the matter could be investigated. Many states have kept such records by noting on the back of the certificates the date of each request and number of copies issued. With the use of microfilm, however, this practice is no longer practical. A new system would have to be developed with the microfilm record.

5. Institute better control over blank certificate forms and forms used for the issuance of certified copies. Most states already exercise some control over these forms, and it would not be costly for all states to tighten up. It will also be necessary for any procedures that are developed to also apply to all local Vital Records Offices.

6. Check the death index for all requests for certified copy in the 20-39 age group (the ages where most fraud activity appears to occur). This suggestion has merit, of course, only for those cases where birth and death occur in the same state but appears to be useful in dealing with the IDI syndrome where death shortly follows birth. This would involve a considerable expenditure of energy at issuing offices, however. A Kansas survey found that 25% of the requests processed were from the 20-40 age group. So the numbers involved may not be small. It is a partial alternative to the interstate birth/death matching scheme.

7. Establish a degree of Federal control over the vital registration system. This could be limited to the enactment of Federal legislation relative to the obtaining, use, possession, or sale of fraudulent or improperly obtained birth records and the establishment of penalties under Federal law. It is not thought that Federal assumption of the states' traditional prerogatives in the issuance of birth certificates would meet with general legislative approval. Voluntary cooperation among states is greatly preferable to Federal mandate.

8. Provide Federal funding for those states willing to adopt recommended procedures designed to curb the false ID problem. This funding would be used by the state in setting up and maintaining those programs.

Since the cost of some of these programs would be quite high, it is thought necessary that some Federal support should be provided.

9. Adopt an Executive Order whereby Federal agencies will accept only certified copies issued by a state Vital Records Office. This would be a means of encouraging states to move toward a system of state certification and away from local certification. Many of the false ID problems originate in local Vital Records Offices. This recommendation does not appear costly.

10. States issue uniform certified copies. "Uniform," in this context, refers to format, information contained, signature and sealing characteristics, paper used, dimensions, color and other physical aspects of the document. Presently, the number of different types of certified copies issued in this country is very high. This makes it difficult to identify a valid certified copy format from an invalid format. Such a recommendation should also include considerations of alteration-proof paper and methods of control. The cost of the program, once the forms are developed, would not be exceptionally high.

11. Set up educational programs for persons issuing certified copies. These programs would concentrate on sensitizing these persons to possible fraud and the means for detecting it. This program would be modestly costly, but could be quite effective.

Driver's Licenses

1. States adopt tamper proof forms with pictures. This would aid in reducing alteration and counterfeit problems. It would be costly for those states (about 20) which have not already undertaken this process.

2. Encourage states to put more identifying information on the driver's license. Many states have recently dropped such items as race, sex, weight, height, color of eyes, or color of hair. These items do help in determining whether the person holding the license is in fact the person named on the certificate. A picture obviates the need for some but certainly not all of this information. The cost of putting this information on the license would be small and these could be of substantial benefit.

3. Establish an educational program for persons giving driver tests and issuing licenses. The program would emphasize the problem of false ID and train

the officials in detecting false ID. Since many of
the persons establishing false identification are
above the age of first driver's permit, the older
applicants should be checked more closely. Also,
this training program would probably be costly but
the results significant.

4. All states should require the applicant to present
positive identification prior to issuance of a
license.

5. Require the verification of the birth certificate
prior to the issuance of any license. This could
not be done at the application stage but would require that all licenses be issued through a central
control office. Before the license would be mailed
to the applicant, the birth facts would be verified
through the state of birth. This procedure would be
expensive but effective when coupled with other
suggestions presented here relative to the birth
certificate.

6. All states should enter into the Interstate Driver's
License Compact and collect licenses held by an
applicant from other states.

Other Comments

This Task Force has looked closely at the two documents emanating from state sources which are of fundamental importance to the commission of false ID crimes. There are many others which are sometimes utilized in establishing false ID and in the subsequent commission of crimes. It was strongly felt that the birth certificate and the driver's license are pivotal because of the "breeder" character of the former and the broad usage of the latter.

It should be reemphasized that neither the birth certificate nor the driver's license was ever intended to be used as an identification document. In modern commerce and business, they have become such to the extent that the overall false ID problem must be considered in that light. It would be useless at this point to say they shouldn't be considered identification documents because their use as such has become so extensive, a fact which illustrated a broad societal need for quick, compact, positive ID of some form.

While the birth certificate is sometimes used for identification, the driver's license is used much more extensively. The issuance by 25 states of non-drivers identification cards has caused the status of the driver's license as an identification document to become even more firmly entrenched. Accordingly, it would seem more logical to work on improving the procedures for issuing driver's licenses and strengthen that document's resistance to fraud and counterfeit than try to change attained public acceptance as an ID.

This would involve two processes: (1) Procedures relating to identifying the applicant would have to be strengthened; (2) The document would have to be made tamper proof and sufficient identifying information would have to appear on the license. In this way, the need for a license and an identification card would be met.

States issuing non-driver's ID cards should also implement stronger controls, as noted above. Since these documents are issued only for identification purposes, it is absolutely essential that their issuance be properly controlled.

Improve the response time of the National Driver Register, i.e., it should go on-line, rather than using the present system of mail response.

YOU WILL ALSO WANT TO READ:

☐ 61048 **NEW I.D. IN AMERICA,** *by Anonymous.* Here is all-new information from a pro on how to get a bona fide birth certificate, passport, drivers license, credit cards, Social Security number — all you need for breaking with your past! You will learn how to project exactly the image you want and then prove you are who you say you are. One of the best books ever written on the subject. *1983, 5½ x 8½, 120 pp, illustrated, soft cover. $15.00.*

☐ 61082 **HOW TO DISAPPEAR COMPLETELY AND NEVER BE FOUND,** *by Doug Richmond.* Heavy-duty disappearing techniques for those with a "need to know!" This book tells you how to pull off a disappearance, and how to stay free and never be found. This amazing new book tells how to arrange for a new identification, plan for a disappearance, avoid leaving a paper trail, case histories, and more. *1986, 5½ x 8½, 107 pp, soft cover. $12.00.*

☐ 61058 **METHODS OF DISGUISE,** *by John Sample.* Need a new look to go with your new I.D.? Everything from "quick-change" methods to long-term permanent disguises are covered in illustrated detail. Disguise yourself so completely even old friends won't recognize you! *1984, 5½ x 8½, 142 pp, profusely illustrated, soft cover. $12.00.*

And much more! We offer the very finest in controversial and unusual books — please turn to the catalog announcement on the next page.

CUID

Loompanics Unlimited
PO Box 1197, Port Townsend, WA 98368

Please send me the books I have checked above. I have enclosed $_____ (including $3.00 for shipping and handling).

Name _____

Address _____

City _____

State _____ **Zip** _____

"Yes, there are books about the skills of apocalypse — spying, surveillance, fraud, wiretapping, smuggling, self-defense, lockpicking, gunmanship, eavesdropping, car chasing, civil warfare, surviving jail, and dropping out of sight. Apparently writing books is the way mercenaries bring in spare cash between wars. The books are useful, and it's good the information is freely available (and they definitely inspire interesting dreams), but their advice should be taken with a salt shaker or two and all your wits. A few of these volumes are truly scary. Loompanics is the best of the Libertarian suppliers who carry them. Though full of 'you'll-wish-you'd-read-these-when-it's-too-late' rhetoric, their catalog is genuinely informative."

—THE NEXT WHOLE EARTH CATALOG

THE BEST BOOK CATALOG IN THE WORLD!!!

We offer hard-to-find books on the world's most unusual subjects. Here are a few of the topics covered IN DEPTH in our exciting new catalog:

- Hiding/concealment of physical objects! A complete section of the best books ever written on hiding things!
- Fake ID/Alternate Identities! The most comprehensive selection of books on this little-known subject ever offered for sale! You have to see it to believe it!
- Investigative/Undercover methods and techniques! Professional secrets known only to a few, now revealed to you to use! Actual police manuals on shadowing and surveillance!
- And much, much more, including Locks and Locksmithing, Self-Defense, Intelligence Increase, Life Extension, Money-Making Opportunities, and more!

Our book catalog is 8½ x 11, packed with over 500 of the most controversial and unusual books ever printed! You can order every book listed! Periodic supplements to keep you posted on the LATEST titles available!!! Our catalog is free with the order of any book on the previous page — or is $3.00 if ordered by itself.

Our book catalog is truly THE BEST BOOK CATALOG IN THE WORLD! Order yours today — you will be very pleased, we know.

**LOOMPANICS UNLIMITED
PO BOX 1197
PORT TOWNSEND, WA 98368
USA**